DOCTORAL DISERTATION

Solving Organisational Development Problem in the Non-Profit Sector-Acase Study of "Holiness Power Bible Ministries"

Dr Osemeka Anthony

AuthorHouse™ UK Ltd.
500 Avebury Boulevard
Central Milton Keynes, MK9 2BE
www.authorhouse.co.uk
Phone: 08001974150

First published by AuthorHouse 02/10/2011

ISBN: 978-1-4567-7450-9

ABSTRACT

Organisational Development is a planned strategy to bring about organizational change. The change effort aims at specific objectives and is based on a diagnosis of problem areas. Planning serves as a roadmap by which the organization can visualize where they are going and how to get there. There has been reluctance on the part of church leaders (Pastors) to adopt formal planning. Reasons for this include a lack of training in the planning process and a belief that planning is not biblical or indicates a lack of faith. The Bible encourages planning and the involvement of others in the process, as noted in the following four scriptural verses: (Proverbs 29:18)" Where there is no vision, the people perish" (Proverbs 15:22)"Without counsel, purpose is disappointed, but in the multitude of counselors, they are established". (Proverbs19:20) "Hear counsel, and receive instruction, that you may be wise in your latter days". (Prov.20:18), "Every purpose is established by counsel: and with good advice make war."Lack of planning is noted in the perceived inability of many church leaders and pastors to meet the needs of their congregation and others ministered to by the church. Poor planning can be attributed as the cause for many churches' failures in achieving their ministerial and organizational goals and as a result, many churches today are facing declining membership and attendance levels as numerous activities divert individuals away from church. Many former churchgoers feel that church is out of touch with them and has not responded to their needs. Organisational development can be used to stem this negative trend. A church should identify the needs of the community; set goals for meeting those needs, and formulate a plan for achieving those goals. The research is tailored in such a way that the following objectives are achieved: 1). To examine the extent planning is being used by "Holiness Power Bible Ministries "to achieve its organizational goals.2).positive relationship between formal planning and growth rates of membership and 3). Finances. Data will be gathered through distribution of a questionnaire, telephone survey to church leaders and pastors and through review of relevant literature. Finally, in my own view I believe that at the end of this research work, the general public with their belief that "Holiness Power Bible Ministeries"will not survive the future challenges would have been proved groundless.

ACKNOWLEGDEMENT

My profound gratitude goes to Almighty God and my Savior Jesus Christ who made it possible for me to complete this course successfully. I am indebted to several researchers, writers who have accelerated the development of the literature on Non-profit sector and Organizational Development. First of all, my parents should accept my appreciation and commendations for giving birth to me and for relentless rearing me to the apogee of their preference, even at death. My special thanks go to Dr Dawn Ring, my academic advisor during my (Master degree, (Counseling Psychology), Atlantic International University), Dr Edgar Colon, Dr Lauran Benjamin and Dr Franklin Valcin, my academic advisors, in (Doctorate degree, (PhD in Psychology), Atlantic International University) for their untiring assistance. I am very grateful to them for the pains they took in reading through my academic course works and ensuring that I get the best out of the my endeavor. I am most grateful to Dr Franklin Valcin for the painstaking in reading through my manuscripts, chapter by chapter, correcting mistakes and at the same time offering me useful suggestions at anytime I deviate in other to bring out the very best in me while writing this thesis. My special thanks go to the Academic Department and Student Services of the Atlantic International University (AIU) for their moral support and encouragement and profitable academic interaction. I must also thank the Financial Department for the "Flexible Payment Plan "and even when I am not able to met up with the tuition fee due to some financial difficulties their tolerance and understanding always boost my morale and determination to persevere. I am highly indebted to Dr Jacqueline E. Edwards, who facilitate my Admission process (Admission Counselor) and mentor who made herself accessible while in her ill condition throughout this course in counseling, Advising and directing me to get the best out of this study. My special thanks goes to Mr Biam (Director Police Pension Office), Mr Esai Dangabar(Director Police Pension Office),Mallam,Atiku,A.Kigo(Director Police Pension Office), Mrs Uzuoma Attang (Deputy Director, Police Pension Office),Mr. John Yusuf(Assist. Director, Police Pension Office) for their morale and financial support and encouragement. I am also very grateful to my dearly beloved wife, Faith Nnenna Osemeka for remaining relatively calm and supportive even when the thesis began to absorb a frighteningly large percentage of my waking and sleeping hours. I thank her for her concern and uncompromising demand for excellence in whatever I do. Finally, I am beholden to my children; Caleb Osemeka, Emmanuel Osemeka, Elijah Osemeka, and David Osemeka for enduring my denial of attention during the period of the work. Notwithstanding the help and encouragement I received from these individuals, imperfections and errors of omission or commission in this thesis are entirely my responsibility.

Contents

CHAPTER ONE

1.0. Introduction

A non-profit organization is formed for the purpose of serving a public or mutual benefit other than the pursuit or accumulation of profits for owners or investors. "The **non-profit sector** is a collection of entities that are organizations; private as opposed to governmental; non-profit distributing; self-governing; voluntary; and of public benefit". The nonprofit sector is often referred to as the third sector, independent sector, voluntary sector, philanthropic sector, social sector, tax-exempt sector, or the charitable sector. "A non-profit organisation can be a church or church association, school, charity, medical provider, activity clubs, volunteer services organization, professional association, research institute, museum, or in some cases a sports association. Non-profit organisations must apply for charitable status to benefit from tax-exempt status and to issue tax deductible receipts to donors. Non-profit organisations are distinct from business organisations which are formed to make a profit and to distribute the profit to its shareholders." The terms non-profit and not-for-profit are often used interchangeably and generally refer to organizations whose profits are not passed on to their members. That is not to say that such an organization is prohibited from carrying on activities that may realize a profit (for example, a church may run a bookstore or gift shop), provided that these activities do not constitute the primary activity of the organization and that the funds realized are used for the objectives of the organization and not passed on to its members."This paper is intended to proffer possible solutions to the organisational development problems in, "Holiness Power Bible Ministries" and hence the choice of the research topic.

1.2. Background of Study

Holiness Power Bible Ministries (abbreviated as the HPBM, and colloquially referred to as "Operation Tikpo ministry) is a Bible believing church, though many people see it as a language church instead of English church because of the word "Tikpo". I will like to quickly clarify the word,"Tikpo" which has generated a lot of confusion in the mind of many sincere seeker of the gospel truth and as a result being discriminated by some people who attached sentimentality in the things of God, even when they know that God is not a partial God. The word, "Tikpo" is an Igbo Language and simply means, "Destroy" in English interpretation. The founder of the church (Holiness Power Bible Ministries) hailed from the Igbo tribe in the eastern part of Nigeria, and south-eastern geopolitical zone. As a group coordinator in charge of the Igbo tribe in Isolo group of district in his former church (Deeper Life Bible Church) in Nigeria and as a prayer warrior is popularly called "praying machine" by some group of friends. In the year 2002, the ministry to **destroy** all the works of the devil, "**Operation**

Tikpo" known as "**Operation destroy**" was committed into the hand of (Pastor, Austin. Udeoha) by God,(1John.3:8) in a retreat ground and having revealed this vision to his (G.O) the General Superintendent of the Deeper Life Christian Ministry, and also known as Deeper Life Bible Church was mandated to carry out the vision as instructed by God. As a result he was commissioned as evangelist by the G.O (Pastor W. F. Kumuyi) to be visiting every branches of the church i.e. DLCM with a view to restoring revival and rekindling fire in the present day churches.

1.2.1. History of Holiness Power Bible Church

Holiness Power Bible Church is the church God has raised to, "Restore the Old Foundation of Christianity" in this present day Christianity. The founder was a successful businessman until when the call came to him for a full time ministerial work. He became born-again in the year 1974 and having witnessed what old time Christianity in the 70's was all about, he quit his business and every other thing in life for his burning desire and passion to save souls which leads to the birth of "Holiness Power Bible Ministries" from "Operation Tikpo power and fire crusade" Which he pioneered in deeper life Bible church for about 2 years, where he served for about 30 years. The founder, left when he was told by God that his time and ministry was over in the Deeper life bible church for his mission (Restoration of old foundation of Christianity) in his new found ministry, "Holiness Power Bible Ministries in the year 2004, November, 14th. Unlike other ministers that left before him, he sought for the release by his father and mentor, who eventually gave his approval and blessing.

1.2.2. Membership:

Like every other newly found churches, many followers initially were from the mother church, "Deeper Christian Life Ministry" (DLCM), while others came from different denominations to join the new church. The researcher became a member of the Deeper Life Christian Church in late 80's after my encounter with the gospel of our Lord and Savior Jesus Christ in a crusade ground where the G.O (W.F.Kumuyi) ministered on that faithful day, 14th, February, 1987. Prior to my change over to the new ministry (Holiness Power Bible Ministries), I have occupied several leadership positions starting from, House leader, Area leader and Zonal leadership in deeper life bible church. My first encounter with this great man of God (The founder) was on September, 2004 in one of the regions "Ajao Estate" where he was ministering on a crusade organized by the region and the message title was "The Fire That Burneth" so when I had about his new founded ministry, the Lord told me to join the chariot and I did as the Lord commanded so I became one of the founding members and the Lord adding to the church as such that should be save (Acts 2:46).

1.3. Organisation of Holiness Power Bible Ministries

The church "Holiness Power Bible Ministries is headquartered in Lagos, Nigeria, where the General Overseer is currently stationed. The days of church activities includes; Wednesdays, Fridays and Sundays. Every Wednesdays are "Operation Tikpo Power and Fire Connection Service, which is divided into two sections, "Morning Section"(8.00am -10.30 am), "Evening section"(5.00pm -7.30pm). Fridays are "Holiness and Heaven Bible Studies (6.00pm -8.30pm). Sundays are, "Sunday Power Services" (8.00am -11.30am).

General Overseer (G.O) was the only one handling these activities. He has no church workers but "Volunteer" from where he picks who and who that will officiate in any of the activity days, his reasons for that was because he didn't want to Lay his hand suddenly on anyone. This lasted for one year before he began to "Ordain Pastors" and "Ministers "whom the Lord called for the work of the ministry. Immediately pastors and ministers where ordained, the G.O in his God's wisdom divided the whole of Lagos state into (Nine) "Regions "namely: 1) .Oshodi Region; 2) .Isolo Region; 3).Mushi Region; 4).Suru-lere Region; 5).Agege Region; 6).Ketu Region; 7).Agegunle Region; 8).Badagry Region and lastly, 9).Lekki Region. These regions were given, "Regional Pastors "who pastor's the church branches in those areas and they are to plan for crusades, see to the needs of their members and also counsel them, though weightier matters are referred to the General overseer of the church at the headquarter.

1.3.1. Sunday School:

Prior to the church service 45 minutes is set aside for "Digging deeper" or what other churches called the "Sunday School." This is meant for doctrinal teachings of the Bible for about 30 minutes and 15 minutes for questions and answers.

1.3.2. Power House Caring Fellowship:

This is where members of the church meet in smaller cells for identification in case there is any problem the leader in charge of that small group will quickly see to that need if it is within his or power, but if not he or she should refer the case to the superior leader for action to be taken immediately and any person who does not identify his or herself with this segment of the church is not seen as a bonafide member of the church. Power house caring fellowship is also the evangelistic arm of the church. Members group themselves together to follow-up each other and new converts and visitors and the resultant effect of this is church increase and multiplication.

1.3.3. Indoor and Outdoor Programs:

The **church** has both **indoors** and **outdoors** programs designed to reach out to the unreached and unrepentant sinners out there in the world such as; **Monthly Power Fire Night** which comes up first Fridays of every month at the headquarter church and **third Fridays of every month** at the regional levels. Quarterly, the church takes it's evangelistic outreach program known as "Operation Tikpo, Power and fire crusade" to the regions and all the souls won in that through the crusade will be handed over to the regional branch church, thereby resulting to church increase and multiplications.

In **summary**, from November, 14th 2004 to 2010, approximately six (6) years now, Holiness Power Bible Ministries has witness a tremendous success in terms of church growth and church planting. Currently, a young church of about six (6) years has nine (9) branches in Lagos apart from the Headquarter church and about 40 branches within the 36 states of the federation including Abuja, FCT, and with overall attendance of about 3000 membership. Currently at the Headquarter level including regional branches, the attendance is between 800 and 900 representing 30% of the total attendance, while the 40 branches accounted the 70% of the overall attendance. In addition to the achievement and success recorded so far is the "Holiness Power Bible Minister's Conference which has been successfully hosted for about three (3) consecutive times. This conference gives the Holiness Power Bible Pastor's and workers the opportunity of meeting with their General Overseer to be equipped spiritually for the work of the ministry in their various states, this comes up second week of August, yearly.

Vetting committee, Marriage committee, and Pastoral committee are the three (3) committees set up by the G.O to look into certain issues and to move the church forward. **Vetting committee** is the governing body of the church, they set out the rules and regulations that governs the affairs of the church, they also look into disciplinary issues, land issues, court issues, and taking strategic decisions in other to move the church forward.

Marriage committee, also play their roles; as the name implies, this committee looks into marriage issues in the church, they guide young men and ladies who are yet to marry through counseling and instructing them on how to go about knowing the will of God in marriage to avoid divorce after getting married.

Pastoral Committee, are in charge of planning and organizing crusade both within the headquarter and the various regions, they also look into the various work areas in the church and recommend possible change to the Vetting committee who will in turn recommend such changes for implementation. Recently another committee was constituted to take care of all crusade nationally and internationally and they are called, **"National crusade planning committee** "they are to plan and organize all national and international crusades. It may interest the readers to know that the researcher is a member of the **vetting committee**, once appointed as crusade director, once a regional pastor before posted to Abuja,FCT, as state coordinator or state pastor and the vice president of the, "National crusade planning committee."

All these were put in place to enhance effective church performance and good administration, and are also intended to ensure there is orderliness in the church.

1.3.4. Holiness Power Bible Ministries

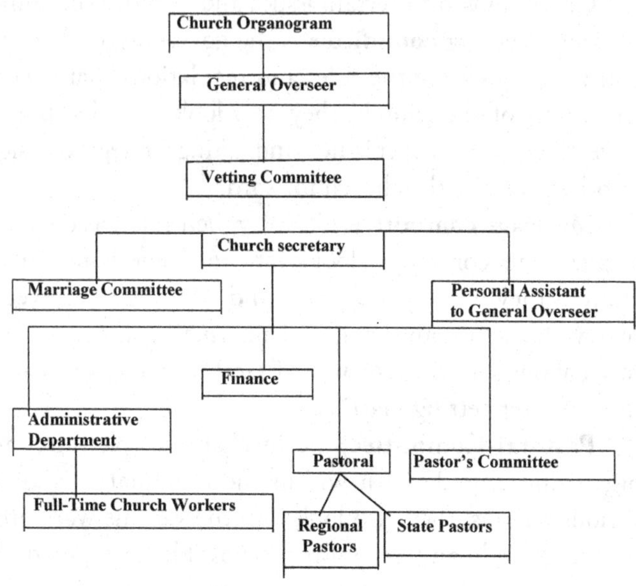

1.4.0. Mission, Vision, Purpose and Goals of the Ministry

1.4.1 Mission Statement

The mission of the church is making disciples: Go therefore and make disciples of all the nations, baptizing them in the name of the Father and of the Son and of the Holy Spirit, teaching them to observe all things that I have commanded you(Matthew 28: 1920a)

1.4.2 Holiness Power Bible Ministries exists to:

- Share the love of Christ
- And Empower people to serve and glorify God.

1.4.3. Vision Statement

We believe God has called us to, "Restore the old foundation of Christianity" (Holiness and Righteousness) through teaching, preaching and caring ministry to reach the unrepentant sinners and to restore holiness back in the life of present day Christians of our generation by providing caring structures for families, providing diversity in worship, providing small caring groups, and knowledge of spiritual gifts.

1.4.4. Core Values of the ministry

- Faith: We are committed to Faith in Jesus Christ as expressed in the Bible
- Prayer: We are committed to continual Prayer
- Worship: We are committed to faithfully offering our worship before God

- Biblical Teaching: We are committed to relevant Biblical teaching that transforms lives
- Small Groups: We are committed to becoming fully devoted followers of Christ through the community of small groups
- Outreach: We are committed to bringing people to personal faith in Christ at any cost
- Giftedness: We are committed to utilizing the giftedness of all believers, men and women, who are called by God.
- Change: We are committed, in an ever changing culture, to effectively present the unchanging Gospel.
- Excellence: We are committed to excellence in everything God calls us to do.

1.4.5. Purpose and goals of the ministry

As a Bible Believing church the purpose of "Holiness Power Bible Ministries" is to fulfill the commission of Christ to "preach the gospel and to "make disciples of all nations," "teaching them to observe all things whatsoever I have commanded you." This constitutes the primary goals of the church, and, as such, represents the very justification and requirement for its existence.

1.4.6. The goals of the, Holiness Power Bible Ministries are as follows:

- To carry out "Operation Tikpo power and fire crusade "in every regions in Lagos state and all the state of the federations on a continuing basis to further the message of Christ.

- To conduct radio, television and other electronic media campaigns on a continuing basis to further the message of the Christ.
- To take, "Holiness power to all the towns, cities and villages in Nigeria and diasporas to further the gospel message of Christ.
- To ordain and train dedicated, and consecrated believers both as full-time pastors, elders and teachers, deacons and deaconesses, and to appoint other officers as required by the church and for the fulfillment of all its objectives, goals, and purposes.
- To conduct, "Ministers and workers conference once every year to train and educate pastors, elders, workers and women leaders on how to be good and acceptable leaders to the people of God to further the message of Christ.
- To educate, instruct, encourage, inspire, and edify those added to the church in all the teachings of Jesus Christ. To ensure that every members of the church make heaven on the last day, which is the ultimate goal of any loving, caring and God fearing pastors.

1.5. Statement of Problems

The subject matter of this study focused on "Solving Organizational Development Problems in Non-profit sector with particular reference to Holiness power Bible Church. Holiness power came on board on the14th November, 2004 with 100 members in attendance. In 2005, a year later the church increased to 300 with an addition of 200 members representing 200% increase in the church attendance. In 2006, I personally discovered that the attendance had soar up to 650 an addition of 350 members representing 117% increase in church attendance and in 2007 the attendance increased to 800 having an addition of 150 members representing 23% increase in the church attendance. In 2008, the membership drop to 650. In 2009, the attendance drop to 450 and in 2010 the church attendance is between 400 and 500 members which is unimaginable. Holiness power Bible Church as a corporate entity and non-profit organisation has its peculiar problem. Apart from the sudden decline in the church attendance and worship, Capacity building is another contending problem faced by Holiness Power Bible Church and other non-profit sectors as they rely on external funding such as: government funds, grants from charitable foundations, direct donations, to maintain their operations, though Holiness Power Bible Church as a new Church (just 6years old) maintain its operations through donations by members and tithes and offering and special contributions from which the church create programs, hire and maintain full-time workers, sustain facilities, and maintain tax-exempt status. Perhaps, this might be the more reasons why the church is finding it very difficult to meet up its financial obligations. Another contending issue is G.O's **"Utterances"** on the pulpit and the introduction of Church **"Administrative Order** "which was later change to, **"Rules and Regulation of the church".** As a minister that declares the word with authority, people often misinterpret his action to be authoritative and disrespect to people, while some are scared by the way he talks including visitors and new converts. The underlying problems are not peculiar to only Holiness power Bible Church but also applicable to almost all the churches in the West African sub-regions.

1.6. The purpose of Study

The need to examine the planned process of change in the non-profit sector's particularly "Holiness Power Bible Church" has become necessary and is considered very germane at this time of our development, re-organization and intermittent metamorphosis, if the organisation (Church) must maintain a standard. We are aware of the current, "Global Economic Meltdown" which has retarded the development of this Nation and thus the need for a long range effort to improve organization's problem solving and renewal processes, particularly through more effective and collaborative management of organizational culture, with the assistance of a change agent with a view of promoting positive humanistic oriented large-system change and improvement in organizations (churches).

1.7. The Research Question

The foregoing discussion has dwelt on "Solving Organisational Development Problems in the non-profit sector" and the need for a long range effort to improve organisation's problem solving and renewal processes. In order to provide the required foundation for undertaking empirical study in the course of this research work, attempt would be made to provide answers to the following research questions:

- What denomination is your church?
- Does the church have a mission statement?
- Does the mission make a difference?
- Does the church structure to fulfill the mission of the church?
- Does your church engage in long range planning?

- Does the church have a formal (written) strategic plan?
- Is there a long range planning committee in the church?
- How long has the committee been in existence?
- What are the weekly activity days of your church?
- What was the average attendance at the largest weekly activities in the month of July, 2010?
- Is your church growing?
- What was the average attendance at the last Sunday service in the month of July, 2010?
- How would you describe the overall change in your church's membership in the last two years?
- How would you describe the overall change in your church's financial condition in the last two years?
- To what extent are the following persons involved in deciding upon overall church direction and expenditures:

1.8. The Research Methodology

Undoubtedly there are numerous ways of gathering data for analysis. Here attempts are made to describe in details the method employed in the collection of data. The specific method to be making use of in the course of this study will include the following:

- Questionnaire Method
- Interview Method
- Telephone survey
- Literature Review Method

The chi-square(X^2) test will be used in this project, because of its suitability to the hypothesis to be tested in the research work. This study investigates the impact of organizational development on non-profit sectors, particularly on church growth, attendance, and financial condition in churches in the Lagos state, Abuja FCT, and Eastern part of Nigeria.

1.9. Statement of hypothesis

For the purpose of this research, the following hypothesis was tested:

General Hypothesis

To what extent does the organizational Development ensure efficiency, effectiveness and improvement of the performance of the non-profit organizations (churches).

This hypothesis intended to detect if really there are tremendous impact of organizational development in improving the church attendance, relationship and financial condition of the church.

Null Hypothesis

Ho:.Churches that practice organizational development experience greater improvements in

Attendance, relationship and financial condition.

H1: Organisational development is best practiced more in larger churches.

Alternative Hypothesis

HA: Organisational development does not make any impact in the improvement of church attendance and financial condition.

1.10. Significance of the Study

The significance of the study is to improve the performance and effectiveness of the non-profit organizations, particularly churches(a case study of Holiness power Bible Ministries) in relation to church attendance and financial condition and the economics importance of church organizations as we welcome the new dawn of democracy in our nation Nigeria and as we put all hands on deck for rebuilding and betterment of a great nation, there is a great need for strategic(long-range) planning for effective and efficient non-profit sector of the economy in this new dispensation.

1.11. Outline of Study

The research project is divided into five chapters, the first chapter deals with the introduction of the subject matter using "Holiness Power Bible Ministries as a case study, purpose and the significance of the study and scope and the limitations. The second chapter review relevant topics to the theme of the project, making references where necessary. The third chapter contains the research methodology of the entire study. The chapter four explained the analysis and the (final) chapter summarise, conclude and make recommendations on the findings.

1.12. The scope and Limitation of the study

The researcher under this section of the project work consider the scope under which this project work revolves as the constraints which limit the researcher's intention to produce more comprehensive and lengthy work. The scope of this study is to "Solve Organisational Development Problems in the Non-Profit Sector in the Nigerian which are very wide in terms of spread as it is peculiar to this type of economy. In order to achieve the main objective of this work, a sample frame is designed to limit the scope to "Holiness Power Bible Ministries headquartered in Lagos and her branches in the South-South, South-East geo-political zone and Abuja,

FCT, where all relevant information needed for this study are carried out due time, cost and financial constraint to meet the said objectives. Above all, this study will serve as informative, educative and useful purpose to all churches and other non-profit organizations, scholars and an insigh for which future research can be based.

1.13. Definition of Terms

For a clearer understanding of the views and analysis expressed in this research work, some words, group of words, concepts and terms frequently used interdependently have been define in this section. Such words, group of words, concepts and terms are:

Non-profit sector: - Non-profit sector is a collection of entities that are organizations and it includes: church or church association, school, charity, medical provider, activity clubs, volunteer services organization, professional association, research institute, museum, or in some cases a sports association.

Non-profit and not for profit:- The terms non-profit and not for profit are often used interchangeably and generally refer to organizations whose profits are not passed on to their members

HPBM:- Holiness Power Bible Ministries

PHCF:- Power house caring fellowship

NCPC:- National crusade planning committee

Digging Deeper:- Searching the scripture or Sunday school

Third sector:- Non-profit sector is often refered to as the third sector of the economy.

DLCM:- Deeper Life Christian Ministry

Tikpo:- Tikpo in "Igbo" vernacular is interpreted in English as 'Destroy"

Organisational Development:- Organisational Development is a "Planned process of change in an organization's culture through the utilization of behavioral science technologies, research, and theory.

Planning:- Planning serves as a roadmap by which the organization can visualize where they are going and how to get there.

Strategic Planning:- Strategic planning is long-term planning process.

References

Aukerman, John H.(1991).Competencies Needed for Effective Ministry by Beginning Pastors in Church of God Congregations in the United States, Unpublished Doctoral Dissertation, Ball State University,

Brown, J. Truman, Jr.(1984).Church Planning a Year at a Time.Convention Press, Nashville.

Clinton, Roy J.Stan Williams, and Robert E. Stevens. (1995). Journal of Ministry Marketing &

Management: Constituent Surveys as an Input in the Strategic Planning Process for Churches and Ministries: Part I. 1(2) 43-55.

Holiness Power Bible Ministries (HPBM,2008).The rule and regulations and administrative guideline.

Maes, Jeanne D. (1998). Journal of Ministry Marketing & Management: I'll Take Parish Strategic Planning,4(1) 25-31.

CHAPTER TWO

2.0. Literature Review

The writers and researchers have covered the topic of strategic planning in the business sector extensively. It is now becoming more common to find writers that have applied these principles to nonprofit organizations, especially churches. (Clinton, Williamson, and Stevens, 1995) found that Strategic planning is becoming more popular in churches as they seek ways to improve their ministries and to provide direction. Church leaders are finding that they lack the skills and knowledge to implement the planning process. (Stevens, Loudon, and Paschal, 1996) found that a survey of church pastors conducted to identify the continuing education needs of pastors in the areas of leadership and management skills identified strategic planning as the highest rated topic. The same definitions of strategic planning that are used in the business sector can be applied to churches. Van Auken (1989) posited that planning is a process of turning vision into reality. Planning is a partnership between you and God in which supernatural power can be channeled through the human efforts of a committed ministry team. Clinton, et,al (1995) describe the strategic management process as it relates to the church as a managerial process that involves matching ministry capabilities to ministry opportunities. Gangel (1989) posited that the only way a church can effectively achieve its goals is if church leaders actively engage in the tasks or process of planning. He also stated "the development of goals in a church or any Christian organization must be accompanied by the development of a plan whereby those goals can be achieved" (p.16).A leader must facilitate the strategic planning process. The pastor, as the leader of a church, is the most logical choice to perform this function. (Bennis, 1985) posited that to be a successful leader, the pastor should incorporate the creation of a focused vision or agenda; clearly communicate that vision and its implicit and explicit meaning, and trust in the vision or agenda as well as the people who can accomplish it. George (1992) posits that the pastor of a church is likening to the CEO in a business organization. The CEO's major influence comes through vision casting. Kegin (1991) posited that there was a significant correlation between effective ministries and pastors who have been trained in and have applied management and leadership skills. Protestant churches (Methodists, Presbyterians, Congregationalists, Etc.) on average lost between one-fifth and one-third of their membership between 1965 and 1990. (Johnson, Hoge, and Luidens, 1993) found that to stem this decline, some of these denominations are giving high priority to new church development, and if these programs are well planned and well executed, the membership loss may be slowed or reversed. Churches that utilize formal planning are finding that growth rates improve as visioning and planning are used. Bill Hybels is the senior and founding pastor of Willow Creek Community Church in South Barrington, Illinois, a church that has seen a 20 percent increase in attendance in the past five years. He holds an annual vision-casting sermon to share the church's vision with the congregation. (Reed, 2000) posits that in his vision-casting sermon, he explained the church's plans for the next 25 years, and how they will reach people locally, regionally, and around the world. This church has experienced first-hand the results of formal strategic planning. The Bible instructs a church to serve in a diversity of activities. The Great Commission directs evangelism; other references mention discipleship, and helping the sick, needy, homeless, etc. (Cheatham and Cheatham, 1995) found that in order to meet these needs, the leaders of a church need to identify or clarify their specific mission. The church has a limited amount of resources with which to address these directives. A church must have a well-defined mission and a set of basic objectives in order to allocate their resources efficiently. (Brown, 1984) posits that when a church plans, it is committing itself to God's work. A church is more likely to have an effective ministry when its members are aware of and thoroughly familiar with the church's 'reason for being.' (Rusbuldt, Gladden, and Green, 1980) found that everything a church does should begin with and reflect the stated purpose of the church. Effective planning is critical to the success of any organization, including a church. (Burns and Hunt, 1995) found that it is well documented in the for-profit sector that formalized planning is an important success factor in goal achievement.

2.1. Formation of Non-profit Organization

An Organisation is born when a group of people work together to achieve a common goal or when two or more people gets together and agree to coordinate their activities in order to achieve their common goals. There is a great deal of misunderstanding about the benefits of forming a nonprofit. Particularly in times of a poor or rough economy, people think they can start a nonprofit to quickly generate income. Or, when people see a strong, unmet need in the community, they often focus only on the singular solution to form a new nonprofit. Before starting a nonprofit business, there is some preliminary "business" thinking that you really should do. Doing this thinking now can save you and maybe your employees and clients a great deal of anguish. Perhaps the best way to really clarify to yourself what you intend to accomplish by forming a nonprofit is to write a basic mission statement for your organization. You'll soon need this mission statement anyway if you plan to incorporate your nonprofit. The following guidelines may be helpful to you when writing your first, basic mission statement.

2.1.1. Basic mission statement

At is most basic, the mission statement describes the overall purpose of the organization. It addresses the question "Why does the organization exist?" The statement can be in a wide variety of formats and lengths, ranging from a few sentences to a few pages. At this stage in the development of your nonprofit, it might be best to keep your mission statement to at most about half a page. When writing the mission statement, try include description of what you think will be the new nonprofit's primary benefits and services to clients

- groups of clients who will benefit from those services
- values that will guide how your nonprofit will operate
- how you'd like others to view your nonprofit

It's often useful to refine the first, basic mission statement by adding or removing a sentence or a word from the mission statement until you feel the remaining wording accurately describes the purpose of the new nonprofit organization.

2.1.2. The phrase "Formation of nonprofit organisation" can mean several things.

A corporation or an organisation that conducts business for the benefit of the general public without shareholders and without a profit motive is known as "Non-Profit Organization."You can be a nonprofit organization just by getting together with some friends, e.g., to form a self-help group. In this case, you're an informal nonprofit organization. An organisation that seeks to do good rather than earn profits must incorporate as nonprofit organization. If you primarily want to make changes in the society, then you should consider forming a non-profit organization (or not- for- profit or nonprofit governmental organization). Nonprofits are focused primarily on meeting strong, unmet social/public needs, rather than maximizing profits.

Nonprofit organization usually should constrain salaries and wages to reasonable amount. So if you are interested primarily in getting rich or making a big salary, then form a for-profit organization.

2.3.0. Various Forms of Nonprofit Organisation

2.3.1. Informal Nonprofit

This is an informal gathering of people organized to meet a usually short-term and local need, e.g, to clean up the neighborhood of litter or to raise funds for a local event.

You usually don't need a lot of ongoing resources for these type of activities.

2.3.2. Nonprofit Corporation

This status is granted by the company and Allied Matter Acts,1990 (CAMA) to a nonprofit organization in Nigeria. People forming a nonprofit corporation or organization usually when they want to ensure that organization is an ongoing entity apart from its members,e.g ., the corporation can have it's own bank account and enter into contracts. Also members of the organization usually are not directly liable for the effects of corporation's operations (the limited liability shield), unless members engaged in deliberate illegal acts for which individuals can be prosecuted. Corporations benefit from the oversight and guidance of a Board of Directors (a requirement of corporations),to some, these lose of power could be a disadvantage. Control of the corporation is vested in the Board of members as a body. The nonprofit corporation is own by the community, not by the founder or Board members. Usually Board members are not paid, but they can be reimbursed for expenses. Employee must keep the amount of their salaries and wages within reasonable limits. Often, a nonprofit must be a corporation in order to qualify for tax- exempt and/ or charitable status from the state Board of Inland Revenue services in order to avoid paying certain taxes and/ or getting donation's/ funds from donors/funders. So you want to form a nonprofit to get donations/funding, you probably should file with your state to be a corporations and will be working for a Board of Directors and you won't own the nonprofit yourself.

2.3.4. Tax – Exempt Nonprofits

A tax – exempt nonprofit usually has features of a corporation (described above) in addition to the following features. The tax – exempt nonprofit can avoid paying certain taxes. This status is granted by State Boar of Inland Revenue services in Nigeria. Usually the nonprofit must be a corporation to qualify for tax-exemption.These nonprofits are constrained to providing services in accordance with their mission to meet the public need (otherwise they have to pay taxes on any revenue over a certain amount). Getting tax –exempt status requires ongoing submission of paperwork to the state Board of Inland Revenue services(SBIR) to retain tax-exempt status.

2.3.5. Charitable Nonprofit

The charitable nonprofit usually has the features of a nonprofit corporation(described above) and sometimes tax – exempt status in addition to the following features. Donors/ funders can deduct the amount of their contributions (to the charitable nonprofit) from their tax liabilities. Charitable status is granted by Inland Revenue services (SBIR) in Nigeria. Usually the nonprofit must be a corporation to receive charitable status. People and funders often are much willing to give money to a charitable nonprofit. These nonprofits are constrained to providing services in accordance with their mission to meet the public need (otherwise they have to pay taxes on any revenue over a certain amount). This status requires ongoing submission of paperwork to the Inland Revenue Board to retain charitable status. Charitable nonprofit must limit the amount of lobbying that they can do (organization that engage primarily in lobbying are usually tax-exempt, but not charitable). There often is strong, ongoing public interest in the operations of organizations, which can result in a lot of effort in the charitable nonprofit to be transparent and accountable for its operations. Often, a major challenge in these nonprofits is to generate revenue from fees because clients often have very limited funding. If you want to form a nonprofit in order to get lots of donations/funds, then you will probably need to be a charitable nonprofit, but you will also have to a Board of Director and you won't own the nonprofit, but the public.

© Authenticity consulting, LLC 3/27/2008

The Internal Revenue Service must approve the tax-exempt status of all nonprofit organizations except churches. Churches are treated automatically as tax exempt without the need to file Form. A vast number of organizations qualify for nonprofit status under the various definitions. Nonprofit organizations include:

- churches,
- soup kitchens,
- charities,
- political associations,
- business leagues,
- fraternities,
- sororities,
- sports leagues,
- Colleges and Universities,
- hospitals,
- Professional associations
- museums,
- television stations,
- symphonies, and
- public interest law firms.
-

NPOs are often charities or service organizations; they may be organized as a not-for-profit corporation or as a trust, a cooperative, or they may be purely informal. Sometimes they are also called foundations, or endowments that have large stock funds. A very similar organization called the supporting organization operates like a foundation, but they are more complicated to administer, they are more tax favored, and the public charities that receive grants from them must have a specially determined relationship. Foundations give out grants to other NPOs, or fellowships and direct grants to participants. However, the name foundations may be used by any not-for-profit corporation even volunteer organizations or grass roots groups. Applying Germanic or Nordic law (e.g., Germany, Sweden, Finland), NPOs typically are voluntary associations, although some have a corporate structure (e.g. housing cooperatives). Usually a voluntary association is founded upon the principle of one-person-one-vote.

2.3.6. Types of Organizations

Nigeria is a Federal Republic. The country's legal system is based on the English legal tradition. The law governing voluntary not-for-profit organizations in Nigeria is a product of English common law. Statutory law governs the creation of not-for-profit companies. Other not-for-profit organizations, such as unincorporated associations, charitable trusts, cooperatives, friendly societies, political parties, and trade unions also exist in Nigeria. Because cooperatives, friendly societies, and trade unions are mutual benefit organizations, they will not be discussed further in this Note, nor will the Note address political parties. Rather, the Note will focus on:

- An association with incorporated trustees; and
- A company limited by guarantee.

2.3.7. Tax Laws

Nigerian companies are taxed under the Companies Income Tax Act (CITA). CITA exempts from tax the profits of companies engaged in certain public benefit activities, so long as the profits are not derived from trade or a business undertaking. Profits of companies established to promote sporting activities are also exempt. Nigerian companies may make tax deductible donations to certain public benefit organizations that are listed in the Fifth Schedule to CITA. Donations made by individuals, on the other hand, are not tax deductible. Nigerian not-for-profit companies are subject to a value added tax (VAT).

2.3.8. Applicable Laws

- Constitution of the Federal Republic of Nigeria (1999)
- Companies and Allied Matters Act (CAMA)
- Companies Income Tax Act (CITA)
- Criminal Code Act
- Taxes and Levies (Approved List for Collection) Act 1998
- Value Added Tax Act (1993)
- VAT Amendment Act (2007)
- Federal Inland Revenue Service (Establishment) Act 2007

2.3.9. Association with Incorporated Trustees

An association of persons, which appoints one or more trustees and pursues registration under Part C of the Companies and Allied Matters Act, is called an association with incorporated trustees. Upon registration, the trustee or trustees become a body corporate and has/have perpetual succession as well as the power to sue and be sued on behalf of the association. There are essentially two forms of associations with incorporated trustees. The first form occurs where the trustees are appointed by any community of persons bound together by customs, religion, kinship or nationality. The second form is identified by the fact that the trustees are appointed by any body or association of persons established for any religious, educational, literary, scientific, social, development, cultural, sporting, or charitable purpose. (CAMA S.673). Individuals not qualified to be appointed as trustees include infants, persons of unsound mind, those who have undischarged bankruptcies and persons convicted of any offence involving dishonesty within a period of five years of the proposed appointment. (CAMA S.675) In addition, the Corporate Affairs Commission, which oversees the registration of incorporated trustees, requires that individuals applying for incorporation as trustees undergo a police background check.

2.4.0. Company Limited by Guarantee

A company limited by guarantee is formed for the promotion of commerce, art, science, religion, sports, culture, education, research, charity, or other similar objects. The income and property of the company is applied solely towards the promotion of its objects. No portion of the company's income or property may be paid or transferred directly or indirectly to the members of the company except as permitted by the CAMA. (CAMA S.26(1))

2.4.1. Common Law Charitable Trust

The unincorporated charitable trust formed under traditional common law rules also exists in Nigeria. A trust may be formed by the settlor inter vivos or by testamentary will. Because the charitable trust is a generic creature of the common law, rather than of specific Nigerian statutory law, it will not be discussed further in this Note.

2.4.2. Unincorporated Association

The Constitution of the Federal Republic of Nigeria states "Every person shall be entitled to assemble freely and associate with other persons, and in particular he may form or belong to "any association for the protection of his interests" (Constitution of the Federal Republic of Nigeria S.40). Thus, with certain derogations, (i.e., those contained in S.45 of the Constitution of the Federal Republic of Nigeria), people may come together to form unincorporated associations. Such unincorporated associations are not eligible for tax benefits. Because the information relevant to making an equivalency determination will necessarily be contained in the governing documents of each unincorporated association, these types of associations will not be discussed further in this Note.

2.4.3. Public Benefit Status

Nigeria does not grant a special public benefit status to organizations that engage in public benefit activities. However, the public benefit character of certain organizations that engage in public benefit activities is recognized through the grant of tax preferences (please refer to Section 5(B) below).

2.4.4. Specific Questions Regarding Local Law (Association with Incorporated Trustees)

No portion of the income and property of a body or an association with incorporated trustees may be paid or transferred directly or indirectly, by way of dividend, bonus, or otherwise to the members of the association. (CAMA S.686(1)) Associations with incorporated trustees may pay their employees reasonable remuneration for services rendered. (CAMA S.686(2)) Active members of the managing council or governing board of an association with incorporated trustees may not take within the organization a salaried position or any other position that is paid by fees. (CAMA S.686(2)(a)) Members of the managing/governing bodies may, however, be reimbursed for expenses incurred in connection with the work of the association and be paid a reasonable rent for properties leased to the organization. [CAMA S.686(2)(b)]

2.4.5. Company Limited by Guarantee

No portion of the income and property of a company limited by guarantee may be paid or distributed, directly or indirectly, to its members except as permitted under the CAMA. (CAMA S.26(1)). A company limited by guarantee may not have as its object carrying on business for the purpose of making profits for distribution to its members. (CAMA S.26(4)]). The CAMA makes the carrying on of business for the purpose of distributing profits an offense punishable by a fine. (CAMA S.26(5)). Any provision in the memorandum or articles or any resolution of the company purporting to give any person a right to participate in the divisible profits of the company other than as a member is void. (CAMA S.26(3))

2.4.6. Proprietary Interest(Association with Incorporated Trustees)

Upon incorporation, the property of the association vests in the trustees.(CAMA S.679(2)). The trustees of the association acquire, hold, and dispose of the property of the association for the purposes of the association. (CAMA S.679(1). The powers vested in the trustees are exercised subject to the directions of the association or its governing council. (CAMA S.685)

2.4.7. Company Limited by Guarantee

A company limited by guarantee does not issue shares (CAMA S.26(2), and so does not create ownership rights in any persons, legal or natural. A company in which persons may be granted a proprietary interest will be designated as a 'company limited by shares' or an 'unlimited company.' (CAMA S.21(1)).Any provision in the memorandum, articles, or any resolution of the company that purports to divide the company's undertaking into shares or interests is void. (CAMA S.26(3))

2.4.8. Dissolution(Association with Incorporated Trustees)

Upon dissolution, an association with incorporated trustees must transfer any property remaining after the satisfaction of all debts and liabilities to other institutions having similar objects. These institutions will be determined by the members of the association at or before the time of dissolution. [CAMA S.691(4)] No property may be paid to or distributed among the members of the association. [Id.] If, for some reason, the remaining property cannot be transferred to institutions with similar objects, the remaining property will be transferred to some charitable object. [CAMA S.691(5)]

2.4.9. Company Limited by Guarantee

Upon dissolution, a company limited by guarantee must transfer any property remaining after the discharge of all its debts and liabilities to another company limited by guarantee with similar objects, or must apply the remaining property to some charitable object. (CAMA S.26(10)).The company or charity receiving the property must be determined by the members prior to dissolution. [Id.] None of the property remaining after a company limited by guarantee discharges its debts and liabilities may be distributed among its members. (Id.)

2.4.9.0. General Activities

2.4.9.1. Association with Incorporated Trustees

The application for the registration of an association of incorporated trustees must state the aims and objectives of the association, which must be for the advancement of any purpose that is:

- religious,
- educational,
- literary,
- scientific,
- social,
- development,
- cultural,
- sporting, or
- charitable.(CAMA S.674(1)(b)

2.5. Company Limited by Guarantee

A company limited by guarantee is established to promote:

- commerce,
- art,
- science,
- religion,
- sports,
- culture,
- education,
- research,
- charity, or
- other similar objects.(CAMA S.26(1))

It is important to note that the Nigerian Criminal Code Act, which is applicable in the southern states of Nigeria, prohibits certain societies as unlawful, based on their activities. Societies of persons are unlawful if formed for any of the following purposes:

- levying war or encouraging or assisting any person to levy war on the Government or the inhabitants of any part of Nigeria;
- killing or injuring or encouraging the killing or injuring of any person;
- destroying or injuring or encouraging the destruction or injuring of any property;
- subverting or promoting the subversion of the Government or its officials;
- committing or inciting to acts of violence or intimidation;

- interfering with, or resisting, or encouraging interference with or resistance to the administration of the law; or
- disturbing or encouraging the disturbance of peace and order in any part of Nigeria.

In addition, a society will be deemed unlawful if declared by an order of the President to be a society dangerous to the good government of Nigeria or of any part thereof. (See Criminal Code Act S.62)

2.6. Public Benefit Activities

The activities listed in the Companies Income Tax Act for purposes of tax exemption and deductibility of donations indicate which types of activities are considered to be of public benefit. These include activities that:

- are ecclesiastical,
- are charitable,
- are educational, or
- promote sports.(CITA S.19(1)(c) and (d))

2.6.0. Economic Activities

2.6.1. Association with Incorporated Trustees

An association with incorporated trustees may engage in economic activities. There is no statutory provision that prevents it from doing business directly or through a for-profit subsidiary. Income derived from economic activities is subject to tax at the regular rate. There are no tax rules that distinguish between commercial or economic activities related or unrelated to the core objects of the association.

2.7. Company Limited by Guarantee

A company limited by guarantee may not be incorporated with the object of carrying out business for the purpose of making profits for distribution to its members. [CAMA S.26(4)] In addition, S.26 (1) of CAMA, requires that a company limited by guarantee apply its income and property "solely towards the promotion of its objects," which must be the promotion of "commerce, art, science, religion, sport, culture, education, research, charity or other similar objects."

2.8.0. Political Activities:

There is no statutory prohibition that prevents Nigerian not-for-profit organizations from engaging in advocacy or from endorsing candidates for public office. It seems possible that the provisions of S.62 of the Criminal Code Act (1) describing unlawful societies could be used to prohibit some organizations from engaging in political activities. Companies limited by guarantee may not directly or indirectly make a donation of property or funds to a political party or association for any political purposes. (CAMA S.38(2))

2.8.1. Discrimination:

Section 15(2) of the Constitution of the Federal Republic of Nigeria (1999) prohibits discrimination on the basis of place of origin, sex, religion, status, ethnic or linguistic association or ties. Furthermore, the Constitution states that every citizen shall have equality of rights, obligations and opportunities before the law. (Constitution S.17(2)(a)] The Constitution requires the government to direct its policy towards ensuring that there are equal and adequate educational opportunities at all levels. (Constitution S.18(1)) The government shall provide free, compulsory and universal primary education where practicable. (Constitution S.18(3)(a).At the same time, the rights enumerated above are non-justiciable. Moreover, they apply only to state actors and do not apply to private or non-governmental entities.

2.8.2. Control of Organization:

In general, no restriction exists on the control of not-for-profit organizations by other organizations or persons. It is possible that a Nigerian not-for-profit may be controlled by a for-profit entity or by a foreign grantor.

2.9.0. Tax Laws

2.9.1. Approved List of Taxes:

Subject to the provisions of the Constitution of the Federal Republic of Nigeria, 1999, the Taxes and Levies (Approved List for Collection) Act 1998 No. 21 ("Approved List of Taxes Law") is the most comprehensive and authoritative legislation on taxes that can be collected by each level of government i.e. Federal, State, or Local Government in Nigeria.

2.10. Tax Exemptions:

In Nigeria, certain types of income are exempt from income tax. Exempt income includes:

- the profits of any company engaged in ecclesiastical, charitable, or educational activities of a public character in so far as such profits are not derived from a trade or business carried on by such company; and

- the profits of any company formed for the purpose of promoting sporting activities where such profits are wholly expendable for such purpose. (CITA S.23(1)(c) and (d)).Nigerian not-for-profit companies may also apply to the President for an order exempting them from all or any profits from any source. (CITA S.23(2))

2.11. Deductibility of Donations to Nigerian NGOs by Individuals and Corporations Based in Nigeria

The laws of Nigeria do not provide for the deductibility of donations made by individuals to Nigerian not-for-profit organizations. Companies are taxed at a rate of 30%. A tax benefit, in the form of an allowable deduction, is available to any Nigerian company that makes a donation to certain Nigerian funds and institutions. Specifically, the amount of any donation made by a company to any of the Nigerian funds and institutions specified in the Fifth Schedule of CITA may be deducted. The amount of the deduction for any year of assessment may not exceed 10% of the total profits for the company during that year. (CITA S.25(3)] The Council of Ministers may alter this limitation on the amount of the deduction by order in the Federal Gazette. (CITA S.25(3)) Institutions to which tax deductible donations may be made include the ecclesiastical, charitable, benevolent, educational and scientific institutions, established in Nigeria, which are specified in the Fifth Schedule to the Companies Income Tax Act. (CITA 23(1)(c)). The Finance Minister is empowered to amend the listing in the Schedule "in any manner whatsoever." (CITA S.25(6)

2.12. Value Added Tax:

In 1993, VAT was introduced in Nigeria; the current rate is 5%. (3)Nigerian not-for-profit organizations are not exempt from payment of VAT. However, VAT will not be assessed on the provision of certain goods and services, including:

- medical and pharmaceutical products;
- basic food items;
- books and educational materials;
- baby products;
- commercial vehicles and commercial vehicle parts;
- fertilizer, agricultural and veterinary medicine, farming machinery and farming transportation equipment;
- all exports;
- medical services;
- services rendered by Community Banks, People's Bank and Mortgage Institutions;
- plays and performances conducted by educational institutions as part of learning;
- all exported services;
- plant and machinery imported for use in the Export Processing Zone;
- plant, machinery and equipment purchased for utilization of gas in downstream petroleum operations; and
- tractors, ploughs and agricultural equipment and implements purchased for agricultural purposes. (Value Added Tax Act 1993 S.3 and Schedule] (Value Added Tax Act and Schedule, as amended)

2.13. Double Tax Treaties:

No double taxation treaty exists between the United States and Nigeria.

Incorporation Requirement for Companies Operating in Nigeria.

The legal requirements for the incorporation of Companies are contained in the Companies and Allied Matters Act (CAMA) Cap 59 LFN1990. The operational requirements of companies are governed by CAMA and several other laws such as the Nigerian Investment Promotion Act, the Companies Income Tax Act, Investments and Securities Act 1999, Foreign Exchange Act of 1995 etc. The requirements are listed hereunder:

2.13.0. Legal Requirements for incorporation of company.

There are several legal requirements stated by the Companies and Allied Matters Act 1990 in Sections 18 to 40 for the incorporation of new Companies.

(A) Name of Company: It is the responsibility of the promoters of the company to select a name for their company. The company must have a name which must not be identical with another registered company or offensive or contains chambers of commerce, Nigeria or federal. Availability must be conducted at the Corporate Affairs Commission to verify the availability and suitability of the selected name.

(B) Registered office address

The company must have a registered business address within Nigeria.

(C) Type of company

The law allows for registration of companies for companies limited by shares, limited by guarantee, unlimited and partnership. Under those companies limited by shares, a company can be a private company limited by shares or a public limited liability company. At incorporation, all the legal objects of the company must be contained in it memorandum and articles of Association. The legal objects are the major business objectives of the company and the framework which it intends to run its business within the acceptance of the law.

(D) Share capital.

There are several types of shares such as ordinary shares, preference shares and deferred shares. The most popular shares are ordinary shares. Non voting shares are prohibited and it is one vote per share except for preference shares. The currency allowed for shares is the Naira. Minimum authorized share capital for private companies is N10, 000, while for public companies is N500, 000. A minimum of 25% of the authorized share capital must be subscribed and paid for. Shares can be paid for in cash or value meaning the directors of the company must have at least 25% of the total issued share capital in terms of cash or property as the time of incorporation.

(E) Objects of the company

The objects of the company must be legal and lawful. Nigerians and Non- Nigerians can undertake all forms of legal businesses. Non Nigerians cannot undertake certain businesses such as production of arms, ammunition, narcotic drugs, military wears, national security etc.

(F) Directors.

They run the day to day management of the company. The minimum number of directors is two and maximum number 50 for private companies. There is no maximum for public companies. Alternate and shadow directors are allowed. The powers, appointment and removal of directors are contained in company's articles of association.

(G) Subscribers.

These are the persons that subscribe to the memorandum and articles of association. They must be adults of over 18 years, of sound mind, not bankrupt, and must have the capacity to form a company. They eventually become directors of the company in private limited liability companies.

(H) Expatriates.

Expatriates are subjected to the provisions of certain other laws such as the Nigerian Investments Promotion Act, Foreign Exchange Monitoring Act 1995, Investment and Security Act 1999, Immigration Act etc.

2.13.1. Required documentation.

Before a company is registered by the Corporate Affairs Commission, certain documents need to be provided by the promoters of the company to the Commission. These documents are contained in section 35 of CAMA. The documents are:

(A)A set of memorandum and Articles of Association of the company (6).

(B)A set of incorporation forms containing the notice of registered office address, particulars of directors, statement of authorized share capital any other document required y the Commission.

(C)An availability of name form showing that the suggested name of the company is available at the Commission registers.

(D)A statutory statement by a legal practitioner stating that all the requirements of CAMA have been complied with.

(E)Payment of the Commission's statutory registration fees of N10, 000 for every N1million.

(F)Payment of Stamp duty fees.

(G) Any other document that may required by any relevant law statute.

2.14. Tax requirements.

(A) Company Taxes.

Under Nigerian tax laws, companies are subject to taxation under the Companies Income Tax Act 1990 at the rate of 30% per annum. There is also Capital Gains tax under the Capital Gains Tax Act, 1990 which is 10% levy on disposal of company's assets. Then there is value added tax for goods and several services including telecommunications which is a standard 5% under the Value Added Tax Act of 1993. Then there is a withholding tax for dividends earnings at the rate of 10% under the Company Income Tax Act 1990. There is also education tax at the rate of 2% under the Education Tax Decree No. 7 of 1993. There is also the personal income tax applied to employees of companies under the Personal Income Tax Act of 1993 charged on pay as you earn basis.

(B) Incentives.

There are several incentives for companies operating under Nigerian tax laws. There is a tax free holiday for 5 years for companies that produce goods considered to have pioneer status under the Industrial Development Act 1990 LFN 579. There is a tax holiday of 100% for 7 years for companies cited in disadvantaged areas under the same Act for pioneer status. There is a tax waiver for 5 years approved status for companies with non resident investment where the original investment was imported in form of equity under the CITA 1990. There is import duty tax incentive under the duty drawback suspension scheme which allows importers claim on refund on duties for imports under the Customs and Excise Management Act Cap 84, LFN, 1990. Investment incomes imported in Nigeria are not taxable if through authorized dealers. There is also capital assets depreciation allowance under the Companies Income Tax Act 1990. There is investment allowance of 10% for companies who incur capital expenditure on plant and machinery under the Finance Taxation Act.Other incentives under the Company Income Tax Act are claims for local value added is 10% allowance for 5 years, labour intensive production is 15% allowance, local content material utilization is 60% allowance for engineering and chemicals, 70% for petrochemicals, 12% for research and development, plan training is 2%, investment in infrastructure is 20% etc.

2.15. Foreign Investment requirements

Under Nigerian law, foreigners are allowed to wholly owed companies or part own companies with Nigerians. The laws that govern foreign investments are the Nigerian Investment Promotions Act 1995, the Foreign Exchange Act 1995, the Investment and Securities Act 1999, the Immigration Act Cap III 1990 etc. Under the Nigerian Investment Promotion Act 1990, non Nigerians are permitted to own businesses wholly or partly with Nigerians in spheres of businesses except production of arms, ammunition, production of narcotic drugs, production of military wears equipments etc. Under the NIPC Act, the said foreign investor is required to incorporate a company under the Companies and Allied matter Act 1990, register with the NIPC, comply with the requirements of the Immigration Act 1990, apply and obtain the relevant license of the sector it intends to invest, apply for business permit, expatriate quota and residence permit from the Federal Ministry of Internal Affairs, apply for all other relevant approvals such as capital importations etc. On repatriation of proceeds from Nigeria, under the NIPC Act and the Foreign Exchange Act 1995, a foreigner can repatriate all business proceeds or even capital income from Nigeria without restrictions. Income earnings can also be repatriated from Nigeria subject to personal income tax and 10% withholding tax on share dividends. Foreigners are permitted to convert their currency and operate domiciliary accounts.

2.16. Voting pattern of private limited liability company in Meetings.

There are no restrictions on venue of Board meetings but it must be held in Nigeria. Attendance of meetings can be personal or by proxy. Then filing of annual returns is mandatory within 42 days after annual general meetings. For private companies, the subscribers to the memo usually constitute the voting shareholders of the company. Except as required by law, voting patterns under Nigerian corporate law are usually by a simple majority, that is a majority of the directors at Board of directors meetings or at annual general meetings of shareholders. However, for special resolutions in matters affecting fundamental changes in the company such as change of name and alteration to Memo and Articles, a majority of ¾ is required by voters in annual general meetings. The procedure for voting at meetings is by a show of hands unless a poll is demanded by the Chairman or a major shareholder of the company or three other members present in person at the meeting. There is also the requirement of issuing meeting notices to shareholders or members of annual general meeting who are entitled to vote.

2.17.0. Incorporation of Non-profit Organisation in Nigeria

Establishing an enterprise entails first a decision on what you want to do, and how. Then, you must decide on the form of the enterprise. Would it be a partnership, a sole proprietorship, a company limited by shares or a not-for-profit organization? Every enterprise in Nigeria is required by law to be registered with the Corporate Affairs Commission, and to comply with the relevant provisions of the Companies and Allied Matters Act, Chapter 59, Laws of the Federation of Nigeria 1990.

2.17.1. Forms of Enterprise in Nigeria

An enterprise may take one of the following forms:

- A Private company limited by shares
- A Public limited company;
- An Unlimited liability company;
- A Company limited by Guarantee;
- A Partnership/Firm;
- A Sole Proprietorship;
- An Incorporated Trustees;

2.17.2. Registration Requirements

The Companies and Allied Matters Act, 1990 [CAMA] is the principal statute governing the registration of enterprises in Nigeria. The administration of CAMA is the responsibility of the Corporate Affairs Commission (CAC), with headquarters in Abuja, and zonal offices all over the country.

2.17.3. The functions of the CAC among other things include the following:

- The regulation and supervision of the formation, incorporation, registration, management and winding up of companies;
- the establishment and upkeep of a suitable and well equipped Companies Registry;
- the conduct of investigation into the affairs of any company where the interests of shareholders and the public so demand; etc.

2.17.4. Types of Companies and Enterprises

Under the CAMA, the following types of companies exist:

- ***Company limited by shares:*** This is a company having the liability of its members limited to the amount (if any), unpaid on the shares respectively held by them.
- ***Company limited by guarantee:*** This is a company without a share capital. It is a not-for-profit company where the liability of its members is limited to such amount as the members respectively undertook to contribute to the assets of the company in the event of its being would up. Due to the tax exemption and other benefits granted this type of company, the **Consent** of the Attorney General of the Federation is required for the registration.
- ***Unlimited Company:*** This is a company where the members' liability is not limited to any particular amount. Each of these primary types of companies may be a **private** or a **public** company. A private company is one,

which places restriction on transfer of shares by members, and limits its membership to 50 persons. It is also prohibited from inviting the public for subscription to its shares or debentures. On the other hand, a public company has no such restrictions as its shares can be freely traded on. It can be listed or unlisted. It is usually listed when it is quoted on the Stock Exchange.

2.17.5. Business Names - for Sole Proprietors, Partnerships & Firms

- ***Business Names:*** This is the name or style under which any business is carried on, whether in partnership or otherwise. The expression firm is used when 2 or more persons have entered into a partnership with a view to carrying on business. Business names are to be registered under CAMA where the name consists of an addition to a person's name. E.g. "John Smith" is not required to be registered, but "John Smith & Co" requires registration.
- ***Sole Proprietorships:*** This is a one-owner business, and should be registered with the CAC as a Business Name under Part B of CAMA.
- ***Partnership/Firms:*** This has the same format as a registered sole proprietor, except that there is more than one person involved. Please note that there is currently (as at June 2000) no provisions in CAMA for what is known as limited liability partnerships ("LLP") as is practice in some jurisdictions. However, the Partnership Laws of most states in the Federation provide for the registration of limited liability partnerships.

Here there are two kinds of partners – the general partners who carry the risk and liability of the business, and the limited partner, whose level of liability is limited to a defined amount. This model makes for better access to finance by a partnership in the sense that a financier could provide capital not only in the form of debt, but also in the form of equity, and since the financier is not involved in the day to day running of the partnership, it becomes desirable to financier that his/ its liability is not open-ended.

2.17.6. Registration of Business Names

The procedure for the registration of a Business Name for use by a "sole proprietor" or "partnership/firm" essentially involves the submission of a duly completed Application Form to the CAC signed by the appropriate persons. This form which must disclose certain particulars must be accompanied by a number of documents as follows: -

- reservation of Name Form;
- the proposed name
- the general nature of the business or proposed activities;
- the full address of the principal place of business and every other subsidiary place of business;
- where the registration to be effected is that of a firm; the present forenames and surnames, nationality, age, sex, occupation and usual residential address of each of the individuals who are
- the intending partners, and the corporate name and registered office of such corporation which is an intending partner as the case might be;

- the proposed date of commencement of the business or activities;
- Passport size photographs or the owners.
- Certificates of professional qualification where the business is of a professional nature.
- Where one of the partners is a non-Nigerian and intends to work in Nigeria, evidence of his immigration status.

It should be noted that additional information and supporting documents may be required in the case of a firm or an individual carrying on business on behalf of another individual, firm or corporation whether as a nominee or trustee and in the case of a firm or individual carrying on business as general agent for another concern or overseas entity and not having a place of business in Nigeria.

2.18.0. Incorporated Trustees:

This is used for establishing not-for-profit organizations popularly referred to as Non-Governmental Organizations (NGOs). It is used for the establishment of social, scientific, educational, religious, cultural and other similar bodies. The organization is required to appoint Trustees who will then be registered as the "Incorporated Trustees of XY Educational Support Foundation".

2.18.1. Reservation of Name:

The law allows the promoters of a new enterprise to apply to it to determine whether or not the proposed name is available for use, and if so to reserve it for a period of sixty days.

2.18.2. Minimum Share Capital Requirements & Disclosures:

The minimum share capital required of a private company is N10,000, and for a public company, it is N500,000. This requirement seems inadequate with the value of the naira having changed drastically between 1990 (when the law was made) and today. The Memorandum of Association of the company must state that the subscribers "shall take amongst them a total number of shares of a value of not less than 25 per cent of the authorised share capital and that each subscriber shall write opposite his name the number of shares that he takes". Taking cognizance of the need for business expediency, the CAMA allows Attorneys, Accountants, to hold shares for promoters, provided the fact of such shares held on trust is disclosed in the Memorandum & Articles of Association. A number of foreign investors in order to expedite the incorporation process, give Powers of Attorney to local professionals to incorporate companies for them and to obtain the relevant statutory licences and approvals for the establishment of enterprises in Nigeria.

2.18.3. One Vote per Share:

Non-voting shares and Shares with **"weighted"** voting rights have been prohibited. All shares (i.e. whether ordinary or preferential) issued by a company must carry one vote in respect of each share.

2.18.4. Disclosures to be published in Company Correspondence and Business Premises:

Every company is obliged to disclose on its letterhead papers used in correspondence, the following particulars:

- Name of the company/enterprise;

- Address;
- Registration/Incorporation Number;
- Names of Directors and Alternate Directors (if any).

This disclosure requirement is a spirited effort to ensure the authenticity of correspondence by genuine companies and as mush as possible to check the activities of fake and non-existing companies. In addition, the law requires companies/ enterprises to display their Certificates of Incorporation/ Registration in conspicuous positions at their principal and branch offices. Non-disclosure attracts both criminal and civil consequences on the part of the company, its directors and other officers responsible for the non-disclosure.

2.18.5. Foreign Companies in Nigeria:

A non-Nigerian is at liberty, and indeed encouraged to invest and participate in the operation of any enterprise in Nigeria. However, the promoters or investors would have to register a company in Nigeria. This company will be a separate and distinct entity from its parent company. Until so incorporated, a foreign company may not carry on business in Nigeria or exercise any of the powers of a registered company. This does not mean however that a company not registered in Nigeria cannot sue or be sued for goods or services delivered. Infact, it can sue and be sued. A foreign investor may incorporate a Nigerian branch or subsidiary of the parent company by giving a Power of Attorney to a qualified solicitor in Nigeria for this purpose. The incorporation documents in this instance would, disclose that the Solicitor is merely acting as an "agent" of a "principal" whose name(s) should also appear in the document. The Power of Attorney should be designed to lapse, thus indicating that the appointed Solicitor shall be cease to function upon the conclusion of all registration formalities. When this is accomplished, the locally incorporated branch or subsidiary company must then apply to the Nigerian Investment Promotion Commission ("NIPC") for a Business Permit, Expatriate Quota, and other requisite approvals and licences.

2.18.6. Exceptions to the General Rule:

Where exemption from local incorporation is desired, a foreign company may apply in accordance with Section 56 of the Companies Act, to the National Council of Ministers for exemption from incorporating a local subsidiary if such a foreign company belongs to one of the following categories:-

- "foreign companies invited to Nigeria by or with the approval of the Federal Government of Nigeria to execute any specified individual project;
- foreign companies which are in Nigeria for the execution of a specific individual loan project on behalf of a donor country or international organization;
- foreign government-owned companies engaged solely in export promotion activities, and;
- engineering consultants and technical experts engaged on any individual specialist project under contract with any of the Governments in the Federation or any of their agencies or with any other body or person, where such contract has been approved by the Federal Government.

2.18.7. Representative Offices:

A foreign registered company can set up a **Representative Office** in Nigeria. However such an office cannot engage in business. It can only serve as a promotional point. Even then a Representative Office has to be registered with the CAC.

2.18.8. Registering a Company: Basic Requirements:

In registering a company the following should be delivered to the Corporate Affairs Commission:

- Availability/Reservation of Name Form
- Memorandum & Articles of Association duly stamped by the Commissioner for Stamp Duties, and duly subscribed to by at least two Nigerians or persons of foreign nationalities who have been granted Business Permit. However, in the absence of a Business Permit a foreign investor could authorize a Nigerian citizen or organization by means of a Power of Attorney to subscribe on its behalf pending the grant of a Business Permit;
- Copy of Business Permit if the subscribers are of foreign nationalities;
- Duly completed Form CAC 2.2/C.O.6 (showing the address of the company)
- Duly completed Form CAC 2.3/C.O.7 (showing the first directors as well as Consent Letters to act as a director, duly signed by each individual director).
- A Statement of the Authorised Share Capital, on the prescribed Form CAC 2.4 and duly stamped by the Commissioner for Stamp Duties.

- Duly completed Form CAC 2.5/C.O.2 (showing the Share Allotments);
- A Statutory Declaration of Compliance by a Nigerian legal practitioner engaged in the formation of the company;
- Bank drafts for the amounts for CAC Filing fees, and stamp duties.

2.19. The CAC shall register the Memorandum and Articles of Association, unless in the opinion:

- they do not comply with the provisions of the Companies Act; or
- the business which the company is to carry on, or the objects for which it is formed, or any of them, are illegal; or
- any of the subscribers to the Memorandum and Articles is incompetent or disqualified; or
- there is a non-compliance with the requirements of any other law relating to the registration and incorporation of companies; or
- the proposed name conflicts with or is likely to conflict with an existing trade mark or business name registered in Nigeria.

Usually, this process could take between 2 weeks to 4 weeks from filing all the requisite documents to obtaining the certificate of incorporation.

2.20. Incorporated Trustees:

Under the Law more especially the Company Law in Nigeria, nonprofit organization (NPO) or Non-governmental organization (NGO) and churches are known as Incorporated Trustees. These means that the Non-governmental organisation (NGO) and all churches are under the protection and guidance of a set of people called TRUSTEES and the Non-governmental organisation (NGO) and church assets and funds are placed squarely under the TRUST, confidence, reliance and dependence of the Trustees to carry out the aims and objectives of the Non-governmental organization (NGO) or not-for-profit organizations including churches.TRUSTEES are different from DIRECTORS OR SHAREHOLDERS in a company because unlike share holders in a company who will do anything to make sure their company derives a profit, Trustees are not entitled to make a profit from the Non-governmental organization (NGOs) but rather to promote the welfare, aims and objectives of the organization freely. Churches are Incorporated Trustees and the Pastors, are the Trustees or part of the Trustees of the Church and they survive through the grants, tithes, benefits, welfare and donations pouring in every time. Many people register Incorporated Trustees in Nigeria to open one Church or the other to make millions, while some genuinely register these Churches to Help people and promote God's words, so it all depends on which Incorporated Trustee Church is helping people and which one is using the donations and tithes to enrich their pockets. Though this is not the major concern in this project.

2.21. The kinds of people that can register Incorporated Trustees include the following:

- Person Bound together by religion, custom, kinship or nationality

- Association established for religious, educational, literary, scientific, social development, sporting or charitable purpose
- Clubs, Cultural Associations, Foundations and Schools

2.22. Examples of Popular NGOs include:

- Nigeria Youth AIDS Program
- Nigeria Youth Working Group on Environment & Development
- Nigerian Association of University Women
- Nigerian Environment Study/Action Team
- Nigerian Institute of Public Relations Lagos state chapter
- Nigerian Integrated Rural Accelerated Development Organisation (NIRADO)
- Nigerian Labour Congress (NLC)
- Nigerian Medical Association (NMA)
- Nigerian Youth Action Rangers
- Nigerian Youth Environmental Network
- NISER
- Obi/Akpor Patriotic League
- Odua Peoples Congress
- Ogoni Youth
- Oil watch Africa
- Olabisi Onabanjo University
- OMEP World Organisation for Early Childhood Education
- Omni Medical
- Operation Happy Home
- Organisation (ACHDO)-Formerly Mother and Child

- Organization for the Advancement of African Women (ORGAAW)
- Organization for the Dev of Sports & Youth
- Orthodox Welfare Association
- Etc

2.23.0. The advantages of Forming a Nonprofit organisation (NPO) or Incorporated Trustee legally

2.23.1. The advantage of Nonprofit organization legally include:

- All donations, aids, tithes, contributions, benefit, assistance, offerings is 100% TAX FREE
- **It is a body Corporate** i.e It has a right to sue and be sued
- **It has a Legal Personality** i.e No one Man can claim it to be its own no matter the amount of Money a person donated. i.e despite the Billions invested by Bill Gates in the Bill gates Foundation, it doesn't belong to him but he can be a major influencial Trustee amongst the board of Trustees
- **Perpetual Succession**: It continues for life and even after the death of the major donors or board of Trustees, it continues with new Trustees taking over i.e if the Principal Pastor of Church dies, the Church continues and a new successor and new board of Trustees take over.
- **Power to Hold Land:** This is a Major factor in being a Nonprofit organisation (NPO) or Incorporated Trustee. The CAC is very particular about Nonprofit (NPO) or Incorporated

Trustees Having the capacity to own lands or buy lands for its operations immediately unless it won't be registered.

- Capacity to own a common Seal

2.23.2. The requirements to register a nonprofit/ Non-governmental organization, churches or Incorporated Trustee in Nigeria

- **Pre-registration Requirements**
- **Select 2 names of the Association:** i.e Incorporated Trustee. The CAC will choose one that is registerable or deny both of them in all its entirety. So choose Carefully. It is very Important to select a Name that is unique and it must end with either the words Foundation, Trust, Organization, Association, Network, Initiative etc (Bottom line it must conform with the practice that is common with Non-governmental organisation (NGOs)
- **Choose the aims and objectives:** of the proposed Incorporated Trustee normally minimum 3 i.e Sample :
- **Address of The Association**
- **Names of the Trustees (They must be 2 or More)**
- **2 passport photographs for each of the Trustees**
- **The personal residential addresses of each of the Trustees**
- **Occupation of each of the Trustees**
- **Tenure of each of the Trustees, the removal and filling of the vacancy of the Trustee**

- **Auditor**
- **Membership**
- **Common Seal** (The seal must be made in Metal that can be inprinted on and must be physically inspected at the CAC
- **List the Executive Members of the association** i.e President, secretary, Financial secretary, auditors etc

The Registration Process.

- **The registration process includes the following:**
- Procuring, Conducting Name Search and Reserving your chosen NGO name (Normally takes 2 weeks or less)
- Filling the Application forms after it has been purchased (Trust me, there are so many forms to fill and sign by all the trustees)
- Advertisment of the name of the NGO and objects of the NGO in 2 National Dailies and One local Newspaper circulating in an Area of the chosen Registered Office where the Association is based e.g Guardian Papers and Punch Newpapers (National Newspapers)
- Ikeja Report or Abuja Chronicle (Local Newspaper) clearly stating the name of the Association and Trustees and calling for Objections from the Public to the registration of the Association
- Submission of the duly completed Typed Application form which should be accompanied by the following:
- Availabity of name Search Report

- A formal letter of Application to the CAC director General stating the reasons why you want to form the NGO and should be signed by either the Chairman, Secretary or the Applicatants Solicitor i.e yours truely
- Copies and Proof of the Original Newspaper Publications
- Two(2) Copies of the Applicants CONSTITUTION (This is the real wahala drafting a constitution). The Constitution must provide for the following:
- Minutes of the Meeting where the Trustees were appointed having the list of Members Present and Absent and showing the voting pattern, signed by the Chairman and Secretary of the Board. The Minutes must be on the letter headed Paper of the Association.
- Minutes of the meeting where the SPECIAL CLAUSE rules was adopted into the constitution of the Association, signed by the Secretary and Chairman showing the list of Members in attendance.
- All Trustees Must attach 2 Passport sized Photographs and one of the passport must be attached to a declaration Form sworn to at the High court by each trustee. This form replaces the State Government Security Clearance)
- Attach the copy of the court registry payment for the Trustee Declaration form
- Trustees should sign against their names on the application forms, state their permanent residential addresses and state their occupations
- Pay all the filing fees at once

It Basically costs above N120,000 and above to register an NGO and churches with all the fees included. It is always advised to add something extra to that fee because of the time and stress involved. It takes days, sometimes weeks to get a perfect constitution without query and it is the most cumbersome thing involved minus drafting the Minutes of the Association. So the price is not static.

2.24.0. Major Problems of Nonprofit Organisation in Nigeria

2.24.1. Background

The Federal Republic of Nigeria is the most densely populated country in Africa. It has boundaries with the Republic of Benin in the west, Chad Republic and the Republic of Cameroon in the east, Niger Republic in the north, and the Gulf of Guinea in the south. National population Commission (NCP,2006) found that Nigeria population is estimated at over 140 million. Yusuf and Schindehutte, (2000) posited that one in every two West Africans is said to be a Nigerian. (Adaya, 1998) posit that the country's GDP is larger than that of all countries in West Africa combined and larger than all countries in Africa except South Africa. Recognizing the indispensable role of small businesses (NPO's/NGO's), and private sector enterprises in general economic development, many countries have instituted enterprise support networks and structures to fuel the development of these enterprises. Nigeria is no exception. (Yusuf and Schindehutte, 2000) found that at various times since the 1970s, the government has designed and introduced measures to promote small- and medium-enterprise development. These measures have included fiscal, monetary, and export incentives. The fiscal incentives included tax holidays and tariff concessions. For instance, small businesses were given a tax holiday for the first six years of their operations. In terms of monetary support, the Central Bank of Nigeria introduced credit guidelines requiring commercial and merchant banks to allocate a portion of their loanable funds to small businesses. Several developmental financial institutions and schemes were also established to aid small businesses, including the Nigerian Bank of Commerce and Industry (NCBI), the Nigerian Industrial Development Bank (NIDB), and the World Bank SME I and SME II initiatives. There were also export incentives from the Nigerian Export-Import Bank (NEXIM) to stimulate export loan facilities to small businesses as well as export duty exemptions administered by the Nigeria Export Promotion Council (NEPC). Other small business incentive programs included personnel training, repair and maintenance of specialized machines, and extension services. Small-business assistance programs have also been established by local and state governments. Over the past six years, government has pursued a policy that should provide fertile ground for small-business including trade liberalization and making the operating environment more friendly to entrepreneurs. (Akwani, 2007) posit that the International Monetary Fund (IMF) has agreed to support more economic growth in Nigeria by helping to finance infrastructure improvements. In the light of these support and incentive programs, it would seem reasonable to expect that small businesses would grow and flourish in Nigeria. However, the effectiveness of these programs remains unclear, and the rate of business failure continues to increase. Accordingly, the present study explores the constraints to small-business growth despite all the programs established to help them succeed.

2.25. Major Problems of Nonprofit Organisation in Nigeria

In almost all economies, NPO's and small businesses are vital for sustained growth. A high failure rate is a huge negative for an economy, especially a developing economy with limited capital. This is the situation in Nigeria despite government programs established on paper to help entrepreneurs. Structured interviews and a survey gathered data from almost 400 small businesses in Nigeria to find the principal constraints to success, including poor management, lack of capital, corruption, weak infrastructure, poor recordkeeping and so on. Unfortunately, many of the solutions are hostage to the political climate as well as educational progress. Harris et al, (2006) found that Small businesses are generally regarded as the driving force of economic growth, job creation, and poverty reduction in developing countries. They have been the means through which accelerated economic growth and rapid industrialization have been achieved.While the contributions of small businesses to development are generally acknowledged, entrepreneurs (NPO's/NGO's and churches) face many challenges that limit their long-term survival and development. (Arinaitwe, 2002) posit that the rate of small business and nonprofit organisation's failure in developing countries is higher than in the developed world. Scholars have indicated that starting a not-for-profit business is a risky venture and warn that the chances of small-business owners including NPO/NGO's and churches making it after the five-year mark are very slim. (Sauser, 2005; Monk, 2000) posited that small business (NPO's/ NGO's church organizations) should develop both long-term and short-term strategies to guard against failure. (Harris and Gibson, 2006; Monk, 2000; Sauser, 2005;

Birch, 1987; Birch, 1981) found that a positive relationship has been documented between small-business development and economic growth in developed countries. However, far less research has been conducted on this relationship in developing countries. (Arinaitwe, 2002) posit that studies in small-business development are necessary in countries like Nigeria because of the dissimilarities in the process between developed and developing countries. It is also essential to understand the problems facing small-business development in African countries because they are significantly different from those facing developed countries. These obstacles include a lack of financial resources, lack of management experience, poor location, laws and regulations, general economic conditions, as well as critical factors such as poor infrastructure, corruption, low demand for products and services, and poverty. Arinaitwe (2002) posit that internal and external components differ considerably among developing countries.

2.26. The significant of studying "major problems facing nonprofit organization and other small businesses in Nigeria.

Literature search revealed that, to date, very little research has been conducted on the growth constraints of small businesses in Nigeria in general and none on this topic. Studies on other African countries may not apply to the Nigerian business environment. Why?

- in a **globalize economy**, there is increasing recognition that identifying the problems facing small-business management in a non-Western context may be meaningful in terms of the types of assistance (finance, training, management, and technology) the West may provide.

- the economy of Nigeria is growing rapidly, and Nigeria has opened its borders to international business. Therefore, scholars and practitioners should understand the level of small-business development, which plays a significant role in providing ancillary services to multinational corporations.
- it is essential to determine whether small-business management practices and policies developed in the West are valid in a non-Western country.
- the study draws management and policy-makers' attention to the urgent need for specific management practices to enhance the effectiveness and sustainability of small-businesses in Nigeria.
- Finally, from an academic perspective this study's insights should contribute to the future development of this line of research, particularly in a developing country like Nigeria. Therefore, the present study is of significant value to practitioners and scholars alike.

Given the importance of small business to a nation's economic growth, and also the role that small business(NPO's/churches and other entrepreneurs plays in poverty reduction, an understanding of the problems negatively affecting small businesses in Nigeria is a vital first step in managing and avoiding the massive failure of these small businesses. Prior research has shown that a number of factors constrain the growth of small-businesses, especially a lack of capital or financial resources. However, the degree to which limited financial resources alone are a major obstacle is still debatable. Studies by Dia (1996), Godsell (1991), Hart (1972), and Harper (1996) found that additional capital is often not required and can be overcome through creativity and initiative. Kallon (1990) found that the amount of capital needed to start a business is significantly negative when related to the rate of growth for the business. (Kallon, 1990) also found that access to commercial credit did not contribute to entrepreneurial success in any significant way, and, if it did, the relationship would be negative. On the other hand, some researchers have argued that small businesses are under-capitalized. Business owners in Africa tend to depend upon their own or family savings, and access to capital remains a challenge. (Gray, Cooley, and Lutabingwa, 1997; Kiggundu, 1988; Trulsson, 1997; Van Dijk, 1995) found that most of them cannot meet the requirements for commercial loans, and those who do find such loans expensive. For example, Kallon (1990) found that 65.6% of the firms studied depended entirely upon personal savings for capital, 10.9% had access to family savings, 9.4% used commercial banks, and 7.8% drew resources from partners, shareholders, and other sources. Keyser et al. (2000) found that in Zambia, a lack of starting capital was a common problem for entrepreneurs, as only 24% received a loan to start their business. Another study by Koop, de Reu, and Frese (2000) found that the amount of starting capital was positively related to business success. In short, research on the role of capital in determining the success or failure of small businesses in Africa is contradictory, thus magnifying the importance of this study is aim to provide a better understanding of the role of capital in the success or failure of small business in Africa. Administrative problems, have been cited as a major cause of failure for small businesses. A study by Kazooba (2006) revealed that poor recordkeeping and a lack of basic business management experience and skills were major contributors. (Lussier, 1996; Mahadea, 1996; Murphy, 1996; van Eeden et al., 2004) found in their studies that inexperience in the field of business, particularly a lack of technical knowledge, plus inadequate managerial skills, lack of planning, and lack of market research. However, these researchers have not identified which management problem or group of problems contributes most to the failure of small business in Africa in general and Nigeria in particular. Identifying the major problem would be a vital major step in addressing the issue. (Kazooba, 2006; Mambula, 2002; van Eeden et al., 2004) found that other negative factors include corruption, poor infrastructure, poor location, failure to conduct market research, and the economy. Practically every African country has its own version of corruption at a great cost to entrepreneurs, the economy, public administration, and society. An understanding of the specific impact of corruption on small business development is crucial in terms of developing strategies to address the issue.

2.27. Economics Importance of Non-profit Organisation

A striking upsurge is under way around the globe in organizing voluntary activity and the creation of private, nonprofit or non-governmental organizations. People are forming associations, foundations and similar institutions to deliver human services, promote grassroots economic development, prevent environmental degradation, protect civil rights and pursue a thousand other objectives formerly unattended or left by the state. The scope and scale of this phenomenon is immense. Salamon (1994) posit that pressures to expand the voluntary sector seem to be coming from at least three different sources: from "below" in the form of spontaneous grassroots energies; from the "outside" through the actions of various public and private institutions; and from "above" in the form of governmental policies.The most basic force is that of ordinary people who decide to take matters into their own hands and organize to improve their conditions or seek basic rights.There have been a variety of outside pressures: from the church, Western private voluntary organizations and official aid agencies. Emphasis has shifted from their traditional humanitarian relief to a new focus on "empowerment." Official aid agencies have supplemented and, to a considerable degree, subsidized these private initiatives. Since the mid-1960s, foreign assistance programs have placed increasing emphasis on involving the Third World poor in development activities. In the last one and a half decade, development actors have adopted "participatory development" as its strategy.

Finally, pressures to form nonprofit organizations have come from above, from official governmental policy circles. Most visibly, the conservative governments of Ronald Reagan and Margaret Thatcher made support for the voluntary sector a central part of their strategies to reduce government social spending. In the Third World and former Soviet block such governmental pressures have also figured. From Thailand to the Philippines, governments have sponsored farmers cooperatives and other private organizations. Egyptian and Pakistani five-year plans have stressed the participation of nongovernmental organizations as a way to ensure popular participation in development. Further, Salamon argues that four crises and two revolutionary changes have converged both to diminish the hold of the state and to open the way for the increase in organized voluntary action.

The first of the impulses is the perceived crisis of the modern welfare state revealed after reducing of global economic growth in the 1970s. Accompanying this crisis has been a crisis of development since the oil shock of the 1970s and the recession of the 1980s, which dramatically changed the outlook for developing countries. One result has been a new-found interest in “assisted self-reliance” or “participatory development,” an aid strategy that stresses the engagement of grassroots energies and enthusiasms through a variety of nongovernmental organizations. A global environmental crisis has also stimulated greater private initiative. The continuing poverty of developing countries has led the poor to degrade their immediate surroundings in order to survive. Citizens have grown increasingly frustrated with government and eager to organize their own initiatives. Finally, a fourth crisis, Solomon is referring to that of socialism - has also contributed to the rise of the third sector. It caused a search for new ways to satisfy unmet social and economic needs. While this search helped lead to the formation of market-oriented cooperative enterprises, it also stimulated extensive experimentation with a host of nongovernmental organizations offering services and vehicles for self-expression outside the reaches of an increasingly discredited state. Beyond these four crises, two further developments also explain the recent surge of third-sector organizing. The first is the dramatic revolution in communication that took place during the 1970s and 1980s. The invention of widespread dissemination of the computer, fiber-optic cable, fax, television and satellites open even the world most remote areas to the expanded communication links required for mass organization and concerted actions. The final factor critical to the growth of the third sector was the considerable global economic growth that occurred during the 1960s and early 1970s, and the bourgeois revolution that it brought with it. It helped to create in Latin America, Asia and Africa a sizable urban middle class whose leadership was critical to the emergence of private nongovernmental organizations. Thus if economic crisis ultimately provoked the middle class to action, this prior economic growth created the middle class that could organize the response. The growth of NPOs operating in the Third World nowadays is enormous. Garilao approaches the causes of this growth by reasoning:

- Societal conflict and tension.
- The need to respond more effectively to crisis situations in the face of breakdown of traditional structures.
- Ideological and value differences with the powers-that-be in the planning and implementation of development work.
- The realization that neither government nor the private sector has the will, means or capacity to deal with all immediate and lingering social problems.

2.28. Nonprofit Organisation: Definitions

In its broadest sense, the term "nongovernmental organization" refers to organizations (i) not based on government; and (ii) not created to earn profit. The terminology of an Non-Profit Organisation varies itself: for example, in the United States they may be called "private voluntary organizations," and most African Non-profit organization's prefer to be called "voluntary development organizations. It is impossible to give one unique definition for an Non-profit Organisation. However, a few have been assembled below for consideration as under:

2.29.0. Definitions of an Non-profit Organisation

2.29.1. World Bank definition of an NPO:

The diversity of NPOs strains any simple definition. They include many groups and institutions that are entirely or largely independent of government and that have primarily humanitarian or cooperative rather than commercial objectives. They are private agencies in industrial countries that support international development; indigenous groups organized regionally or nationally; and member-groups in villages. NPOs include charitable and religious associations that mobilize private funds for development, distribute food and family planning services and promote community organization. They also include independent cooperatives, community associations, water-user societies, women groups and pastoral associations. Citizen Groups that raise awareness and influence policy are also NPOs." A non-profit making, voluntary, service-oriented/development oriented organization, either for the benefit of members (a grassroots organization) or of other members of the population (an agency).

- It is an organization of private individuals who believe in certain basic social principles and who structure their activities to bring about development to communities that they are servicing.
- Social development organization assisting in empowerment of people.
- An organization or group of people working independent of any external control with specific objectives and aims to fulfil tasks that

are oriented to bring about desirable change in a given community or area or situation.

- An organization not affiliated to political parties, generally engaged in working for aid, development and welfare of the community.
- Organization committed to the root causes of the problems trying to better the quality of life especially for the poor, the oppressed, the marginalized in urban and rural areas.
- Organizations established by and for the community without or with little intervention from the government; they are not only a charity organization, but work on socio-economic-cultural activities.
- An organization that is flexible and democratic in its organization and attempts to serve the people without profit for itself.

2.30. Typologies of NPOs

A number of people have sought to categorize NPOs into different types. Some typologies distinguish them according to the focus of their work for instance whether it is primarily service- or welfare-oriented or whether it is more concerned with providing education and development activities to enhance the ability of the poorest groups to secure resources. Such organizations are also classified according to the level at which they operate, whether they collaborate with self-help organizations (i.e. community-based organizations), whether they are federations of such organizations or whether they are themselves a self-help organization. They can also be classified according to the approach they undertake, whether they operate projects directly or focus on tasks such as advocacy and networking.

- **Relief and Welfare Agencies**: such as missionary societies.
- **Technicalinnovation organizations**: organizations that operate their own projects to pioneer new or improved approaches to problems, generally within a specific field.
- **Public Service contractors**: NPOs mostly funded by Northern governments that work closely with Southern governments and official aid agencies. These are contracted to implement components of official programs because of advantages of size and flexibility.
- **Popular development agencies**: both Northern and Southern NPOs that concentrate on self-help, social development and grassroots democracy.
- **Grassroot development organizations**: Southern locally-based development NGOs whose members are poor or oppressed themselves, and who attempt to shape a popular development process (these often receive funding from Development Agencies).
- **Advocacy groups and networks**: organizations without field projects that exist primarily for education and lobbying.

2.31.0. Typology of NPOs

2.31.1. NPO types by orientation:

- Charitable Orientation often involves a top-down paternalistic effort with little participation by the "beneficiaries". It includes NPOs with activities directed toward meeting the needs of the poor -distribution of food, clothing or medicine; provision of housing, transport, schools etc. Such NPOs may also undertake relief activities during a natural or man-made disaster.
- Service Orientation includes NPOs with activities such as the provision of health, family planning or education services in which the program is designed by the NPO and people are expected to participate in its implementation and in receiving the service.
- Participatory Orientation is characterized by self-help projects where local people are involved particularly in the implementation of a project by contributing cash, tools, land, materials, labor etc. In the classical community development project, participation begins with the need definition and continues into the planning and implementation stages. Cooperatives often have a participatory orientation.
- Empowering Orientation is where the aim is to help poor people develop a clearer understanding of the social, political and economic factors affecting their lives, and to strengthen their awareness of their own potential power to control their lives. Sometimes, these groups

develop spontaneously around a problem or an issue, at other times outside workers from NPOs play a facilitating role in their development. In any case, there is maximum involvement of the people with NPOs acting as facilitators.

(b) NPO Types by level of operation:

- Community-based Organizations (CBOs) arise out of people own initiatives. These can include sports clubs, women organizations, neighborhood organizations, religious or educational organizations. There are a large variety of these, some supported by NPOs, national or international NPOs, or bilateral or international agencies, and others independent of outside help. Some are devoted to rising the consciousness of the urban poor or helping them to understand their rights in gaining access to needed services while others are involved in providing such services.
- Citywide Organizations include organizations such as chambers of commerce and industry, coalitions of business, ethnic or educational groups and associations of community organizations. Some exist for other purposes, and become involved in helping the poor as one of many activities, while others are created for the specific purpose of helping the poor.
- National NPOs include organizations such as the Red Cross, professional organizations etc. Some of these have state and city branches and assist local NPOs.
- International NPOs range from secular agencies such as Redda BArna and Save the Children organizations, OXFAM, CARE, Ford and

Rockefeller Foundations to religiously motivated groups. Their activities vary from mainly funding local NPOs, institutions and projects, to implementing the projects themselves.

2.32.0. Roles of NPOs

Among the wide variety of roles that NPOs play, Cousins identified six important roles:

2.32.1. Roles of NPOs

- **Development and Operation of Infrastructure**: Community-based organizations and co-operatives can acquire, subdivide and develop land, construct housing, provide infrastructure and operate and maintain infrastructure such as wells or public toilets and solid waste collection services. They can also develop building material supply centers and other community-based economic enterprises. In many cases, they will need technical assistance or advice from governmental agencies or higher-level NPOs.
- **Supporting Innovation, Demonstration and Pilot Projects**: NPO have the advantage of selecting particular places for innovative projects and specify in advance the length of time which they will be supporting the project - overcoming some of the shortcomings that governments face in this respect. NPOs can also be pilots for larger government projects by virtue of their ability to act more quickly than the government bureaucracy.
- **Facilitating Communication**: NPOs use interpersonal methods of communication,

and study the right entry points whereby they gain the trust of the community they seek to benefit. They would also have a good idea of the feasibility of the projects they take up.

- The significance of this role to the government is that NPOs can communicate to the policy-making levels of government, information about the lives, capabilities, attitudes and cultural characteristics of people at the local level. NPOs can facilitate communication upward from people to the government and downward from the government to the people. Communication upward involves informing government about what local people are thinking, doing and feeling while communication downward involves informing local people about what the government is planning and doing. NPOs are also in a unique position to share information horizontally, networking between other organizations doing similar work.
- **Technical Assistance and Training:** Training institutions and NPOs can develop a technical assistance and training capacity and use this to assist both CBOs and governments.
- **Research, Monitoring and Evaluation:** Innovative activities need to be carefully documented and shared - effective participatory monitoring would permit the sharing of results with the people themselves as well as with the project staff.
- **Advocacy for and with the Poor:** In some cases, NPOs become spokespersons or ombudsmen for the poor and attempt to influence government policies and programs on their behalf. This

may be done through a variety of means ranging from demonstration and pilot projects to participation in public forums and the formulation of government policy and plans, to publicizing research results and case studies of the poor. Thus NPOs play roles from advocates for the poor to implementers of government programs; from agitators and critics to partners and advisors; from sponsors of pilot projects to mediators.

2.33. Role of NPOs/NGOs in Today's Globalizing World

NPOs nationally and internationally indeed have a crucial role in helping and encouraging governments into taking the actions to which they have given endorsement in international fora. Increasingly, NPOs are able to push around even the largest governments. NPOs are now essentially important actors before, during, and increasingly after, governmental decision-making sessions. The UN Secretary-General in 1995 stated that "Non-governmental organizations are a basic element in the representation of the modern world. And their participation in international organizations is in a way a guarantee of the latter political legitimacy. On all continents non-governmental organizations are today continually increasing in number. And this development is inseparable from the aspiration to freedom and democracy which today animates international society.From the standpoint of global democratization, we need the participation of international public opinion and the mobilizing powers of non-governmental organizations". NPOs are facing a challenge to organize themselves to work in more global and strategic ways in the future. They must build outwards from concrete innovations at grassroots level to connect with the forces that influence patterns of poverty, prejudice and violence: exclusionary economics, discriminatory politics, selfish and violent personal behavior, and the capture of the world of knowledge and ideas by elites. In a sense this is what NPOs are already doing, by integrating micro and macro-level action in their project and advocacy activities. "Moving from development as delivery to development as leverage is the fundamental change that characterizes this shift, and it has major implications for the ways in which NPOs organize themselves, raise and spend their resources, and relate to others." In the dynamic environment, NPOs need to find methods of working together through strategic partnerships that link local and global processes together.

By sinking roots into their own societies and making connections with others inside and outside civil society, NPOs can generate more potential to influence things where it really matters because of the multiple effects that come from activating a concerned society to work for change in a wider range of settings. The small size and limited financial resources of most NPOs make them unlikely challengers of economic and political systems sustained by the interests of big government and big businesses. However, the environment, peace, human rights, consumer rights and women movements provide convincing examples of the power of voluntary action to change society. This seeming paradox can be explained by the fact that the power of voluntary action arises not from the size and resources of individual voluntary organizations, but rather from the ability of the voluntary sector to coalesce the actions of hundreds, thousands, or even millions of citizens through vast and constantly evolving networks that commonly lack identifiable structures, embrace many chaotic and conflicting tendencies, and yet act as if in concert to create new political and institutional realities". These networks are able to encircle, infiltrate, and even co-opt the resources of opposing bureaucracies. They reach across sectors to intellectuals, press, community organizations. Once organized, they can, through electronic communications, rapidly mobilize significant political forces on a global scale.

2.34. Role of NGOs in Development Cooperation

The essence of nongovernmental organizations remains the same: to provide basic services to those who need them. Many NPOs have demonstrated an ability to reach poor people, work in inaccessible areas, innovate, or in other ways achieve things better than by official agencies. Many NPOs have close links with poor communities. Some are membership organizations of poor or vulnerable people; others are skilled at participatory approaches. Their resources are largely additional; they complement the development effort of others, and they can help to make the development process more accountable, transparent and participatory. They not only "fill in the gaps" but they also act as a response to failures in the public and private sectors in providing basic services. Mirroring the support given to northern NPOs, official funding of southern NPOs has taken two forms: the funding of initiatives put forward by southern NPOs, and the utilization of the services of southern NPOs to help donors achieve their own aid objectives. Donor funding of southern NPOs has received a mixed reception from recipient governments. Clear hostility from many non-democratic regimes has been part of more general opposition to any initiatives to support organizations beyond the control of the state. But even in democratic countries, governments have often resisted moves seen as diverting significant amounts of official aid to non-state controlled initiatives, especially where NGO projects have not been integrated with particular line ministry programs. The common ground between donors and NPOs can be expected to grow, especially as donors seek to make more explicit their stated objectives of enhancing democratic processes and strengthening marginal groups in civil society. However, and in spite of a likely expansion and deepening of the reverse agenda, NPOs are likely to maintain their wariness of too close and extensive an alignment with donors.

2.35. Interactions with Formal Private Sector

Nonprofit Organisation's vary greatly in the extent to which they ensure beneficiary participation within their own programs. At one extreme are Nonprofit Organisations whose orientation and competence are very similar to the private sector firms with whom they compete for contracts in project implementation or service delivery. (Steinberg, 1987) posit that the nonprofit sector as a whole competes with the for-profit sector for skilled labor, sales, and reduced cost services provision. Such Nonprofit Organisations may be very efficient (and in strong demand) as service deliverers but are oriented to meeting the requirements of bureaucratic funding agencies and are unlikely to use participatory processes. At the other extreme are participatory nonprofit oganiPOs which see themselves exclusively as enablers and capacity builders and refuse to compromise their objectives or independence by collaborating in official programs. These NPOs usually do not interact much with the formal private sector. There is a lot of mutual distrust and misunderstandings between these two sectors. Often they both see only negative sides of another party existence.

The formal private sector considers NPOs shallow and irresponsible, while the informal private sector often looks at for-profit organizations as greedy and selfish entities.

2.36. Interactions with the State

As it is mentioned already, one of the fundamental reasons that NPOs have received so much attention of late is that they are perceived to be able to do something that national governments cannot or will not do. However, it is important to recognize that relations between NPOs and governments vary drastically from region to region and country to country. For example, NPOs in India derive much support and encouragement from their government and tend to work in close collaboration with it. NPOs from Africa also acknowledged the frequent need to work closely with their government or at least avoid antagonizing the authorities. Most NPOs from Latin America offered a much different perspective: NGOs and other grassroots organizations as an opposition to government. In the Third World, the difficult economic situation may force governments to yield to pressure from multilateral agencies to give money to NPOs. In these cases, the governments act as conduits of funds but is some cases try to maintain control over these NPOs precisely because of their access to funds. However, it was also recognized that through the multilateral donors, NGO cooperation and solidarity can influence policy at the national levels. Multilateral donors may serve as a kind of "buffer" between government and NPOs in order to avoid unnecessary current tensions and to promote coherent national development strategies.

2.37. A Healthy State-Non-profit Organisation Relationship

A healthy relationship is only conceivable when both parties share common objectives. If the government commitment to improving of the provision of urban services is weak, Nonprofit Organisations will find dialogue and collaboration frustrating or even counter-productive. Likewise, repressive governments will be wary of Nonprofit Organisations which represent the poor or victimized. Where government has a positive social agenda (or even where individual ministries do) and where Non-profit Organisations are effective, there is the potential for a strong, collaborative relationship. This does not mean the sub-contracting of placid Nonprofit Organisations, but a "genuine partnership between Nonprofit Organisations and the government to work on a problem facing the country or a region... based on mutual respect, acceptance of autonomy, independence, and pluralism of Nonprofit Organisation opinions and positions."However, as Tandon points out, such relations are rare, even when the conditions are met. The mutual distrust and jealousy appears to be deep-rooted. Governments fear that Nonprofit Organisations erode their political power or even threaten national security. And Nonprofit Organisations mistrust the motivation of the government and its officials. Though controversial and risky, many of the more strategic Nonprofit Organisations are overcoming their inhibitions and are seeking closer collaboration with governments. However, with closer collaboration comes increased risk of corruption, reduced independence, and financial dependency.

2.38.0. Fostering an Enabling Environment

(Brown 1990) posit that the state has various instruments it can use, for good or ill, to influence the health of the NPO sector. The level of response can be non-interventionist, active encouragement, partnership, co-option or control.

2.38.1. Ingredients of an enabling policy environment

- "Good Governance" - social policies which encourage a healthy civil society and public accountability of state institutions.
- Regulations - designed to help, not hinder, NPO growth, but also to root out corruption and to foster sound management discipline; eliminate restrictive laws and procedures.
- Taxation policies - to provide incentives for activities which conform with State development priorities; to encourage indigenous philanthropy and income generation.
- Project/Policy implementation - State-NPO collaboration with proven NPOs in a way which allows the NPOs to remain true to their agenda and accountable to members or their traditional constituency. This might typically indicate the following roles for NPOs within government: articulation of beneficiaries needs to project authorities, providing information about the scheme to communities, organizing communities to take advantage of the scheme benefits, delivering services to less accessible populations, serving as intermediaries to other NPOs.

- Policy formulation - provision of information to NPOs for dissemination to their constituencies; offering a role to NPOs in public consultations; invitation to NPO leaders to serve on official commissions etc. (for example, the Indian NPO, DISHA, has been an influential member of the Central Government Commission on bonded labor). Public access to information is the key to success in this area.
- Coordination - where the government fosters but does not dominate coordination, for example, through having NPO Units in relevant line ministries or NPO consultative committees; NPOs would be encouraged to attend to geographic or sectoral gaps, to avoid religious or ethnic bias, to avoid activities which contradict state programs or
- which make unrealistic promises; the government encourages training of NPO staff, for example, by ensuring that its own training institutions offer courses of relevance to

NPOs; the government encourages improved attention to management skills, strategic planning and sharing of experience within the sector.

- Official support - the government provides funds, contracts and training opportunities to give special encouragement to NPO activities in priority areas without undermining NPOs autonomy and independence; broad agreement is sought with NPOs on such priorities by establishing formal consultation with NPO leaders. Fora such as the Council for Advancement of People Action and Rural Technology (the body which channels government funds to NPOs in India) and the forthcoming Community Action Program (a local government scheme for financing NPOs and community initiatives in Uganda) are illustrations.

For individual NPOs, the most favorable policy setting is when legal restrictions are minimized, when they have complete freedom to receive funds from whomsoever they choose, to speak out as they wish and to associate freely with whoever they select. In such a setting, the NPO sector is likely to grow most rapidly, but "bigger" does not necessarily mean "better." Loose regulations and reporting open the door for unhealthy and even corrupt NPO activities which may taint the sector as a whole. Where the expansion of the sector has been most rapid (e.g. South Asia and certain African countries) there is considerable concern about the rapid ascension of "bogus" NPOs - NPOs which serve their own interest rather than those of vulnerable groups. The individual NGOs may be healthy, but collectively there may be insufficient coordination, duplication of effort, and important gaps left unaddressed.

2.39. Nonprofit Organisation Accountability

The final important aspect of the role of NPOs in developmental process, i.e. providing basic services, is their accountability. Concerns about NPO accountability have been raised by a number of NPO scholars. Najam (1996) in his conceptual framework for NPO accountability distinguishes three categories of accountability considerations:

NPO accountability to patrons.

NPO accountability to clients.

NPO accountability to themselves.

NPO accountability to patrons

The most obvious NPO-patron relationship would be that between NPOs and donors. Donors may be both external (for example, governments, foundations, or other NPOs) and internal (members who contribute smaller amounts). NPO-patron relationships have very clear, though unwritten, lines of responsibility. The mechanisms for enforcing accountability tend to be strong: grants are cancelled, membership dues dwindle, accreditations are revoked, and collaborative agreements are reconsidered. In many cases, however, the critical danger may be not a lack of NPO accountability or mechanisms of enforcing accountability, but a danger of being coerced, or what may be called the "puppetisation" of NPOs. The rise of quasi NPOs caused by "donor dependency" (especially of foreign patrons) some times is viewed as a danger to a national security and an external attack on local priorities, culture and values.

2.40. Nonprofit Organisation accountability to clients

The obvious line of responsibility is for the NGO to be accountable to the needs and aspirations of the community it is working with. Basically, serving community interests is the stated primary goal of much NGO activity in development. Often in practice, not only do impoverished communities lack mechanisms of holding NGOs accountable; the process of aspiration definition is also often murky and subjective. Unlike donors, communities cannot withdraw their funding; unlike governments, they cannot impose conditionalities.

2.41. Nonprofit Oraginsation accountability to themselves

This kind of responsibility manifests itself on several levels. NPOs are ultimately responsible to the vision that made them NPOs in the first place. They are responsible to their stated mission, to their staff, to their supporters/ members, to their coalition partners, to their larger constituency, and finally to the NPO community at large. Obviously, the specific counters of accountability to themselves are likely to be different for membership and non-membership organizations. For individual NPOs, the most favorable policy setting is when legal restrictions are minimized, when they have complete freedom to receive funds from whomsoever they choose, to speak out as they wish and to associate freely with whoever they select. In such a setting, the NPO sector is likely to grow most rapidly, but "bigger" does not necessarily mean "better." Loose regulations and reporting open the door for unhealthy and even corrupt NPO activities which may taint the sector as a whole. Where the expansion of the sector has been most rapid (e.g. South Asia and certain African countries) there is considerable concern about the rapid ascension of "bogus" NPOs - NPOs which serve their own interest rather than those of vulnerable groups. The individual NPOs may be healthy, but collectively there may be insufficient coordination, duplication of effort, and important gaps left unaddressed.

2.42. General Levels of NPO Accountability: A Tentative Assessment

2.43. NPO Roles in the Project Cycle

<Image 2.42>

Accountability category	Functional Accountability	Strategic Accountability
To patrons	High	Medium
To clients	Low-Nil	Nil
To themselves	Low	Low

<image 2.43>

Stage in Project Cycle	Potential NPO Involvement
Project Identification	provide advice/information on local conditions participate in environmental and social assessments organize consultations with beneficiaries/affected parties transmit expressed needs/priorities of local communities to project staff act as a source, model or sponsor of project ideas implement pilot projects
Project Design	consultant to the government, to local communities assist in promoting a participatory approach to project design channel information to local populations
Financing	co-financier (in money or in kind) of a project component source of funds for activities complementary to the proposed donor-financed project
Implementation	project contractor or manager (for delivery of services, training, construction, etc.) promote community participation in project activities financial intermediary role supplier of technical knowledge to local beneficiaries

Nonprofit Organisations can serve as enablers of the partnership through setting cooperation frameworks. Nonprofit Organisations, through community education, can awaken latent local champions that would act as representatives of a community, take over the leadership role and push through the partnership. Nonprofit Organisations can ensure that the goals of the major stakeholders are mutually compatible and understood by the sides. They can provide capacity building of all stakeholders. The community and its representatives and intermediaries such as NPOs can play a major role in awareness-raising, advocacy, decision making, implementing and of course in operations and maintenance of the infrastructure facilities. Nonprofit Organisations can ensure the quality of services provided by either public or private sector and monitor the price. Nonprofit Organisations may ensure transparency and that the interests of all the major stakeholders are reflected in project development. There is especially important since they usually pay special attention to meeting the needs of the poor. Nonprofit Organisations are by their nature very flexible. This quality is extremely important for long-term, capital intensive projects, changes in investment plans, technology choices and priority actions. Nonprofit Organisations have a system that will quickly respond to unforeseen circumstances. Partnerships with Nonprofit Organisations involvement can reduce construction costs, increase cost recovery, promote sustainability and respond more to the need of the users.

2.44.0. Organisational Development

2.44.1. Description

An Organization Development practitioner is to an organization as a physician is to a human body. The practitioner "diagnoses" (or discovers) the most important priorities to address in the organization, suggests a change-management plan, and then guides the organization through the necessary change. The system of organizations is very similar, if not the same as, the system of human beings after all, organizations are made up of humans! Therefore, when trying to understand the field of organization development, it might be useful to compare aspects of the field of organization development to aspects of the field of medicine. For example, the study of the theories and structures of organizations (often in courses called "organizational theory") is similar to the study of anatomy and physiology of human systems. Similarly, the study of organizational behavior is similar to the study of psychology and sociology in human systems. Finally, the study and field of organization development compares to the study and field of medicine regarding human systems. That is, in OD, practitioners work in a manner similar to "organizational physicians" intending to improve the effectiveness of people and organizations by:

- Establishing relationships with key personnel in the organization (often called "entering" and "contracting" with the organization);
- Researching and evaluating systems in the organization to understand dysfunctions and/or goals of the systems in the

organization ("diagnosing" the systems in the organization);

- Identifying approaches (or "interventions") to improve effectiveness of the organization and its people;
- Applying approaches to improve effectiveness (methods of "planned change" in the organization),
- Evaluating the ongoing effectiveness of the approaches and their results.
-

There are different definitions and views on how the change should occur. The nature and needs of organizations are changing dramatically. Correspondingly, the profession of organization development (OD) has been changing to meet the changing needs of organizations. Therefore, it may be most useful to consider several definitions of organization development.

2.45. Definitions of Organization Development

Fundamentally, OD is the implementation of a process of planned (as opposed to unplanned) change for the purpose of organizational improvement (as opposed to a focus solely on performance). It is rooted in the social and behavioral sciences and draw its influences from a wide variety of content areas, including social psychology, group dynamics, industrial organizational(I/O) Psychology, participative management theory, organizational behavior, sociology, and even psychotherapy. This diverse background has been cited as both strength and a weakness of OD. Its strength lies in the breadth and diversity that such openness affords. For the most part, all one needs to do to join a national network of OD professionals is to agree to abide by set of stated principles and values; no specific test of skills or knowledge are required. It is unlikely, for example, that a more restrictive or narrowly focused profession could yield practitioners specializing in one-on –one coaching using multisource feedback and large-scale interventions with five hundred or more executive in the same room at the same time. Such openness to new perspectives, approaches, and experiences as being equally representative of OD work, however, is seen by many as a weakness of the field as well. The lack of set boundaries contributes significantly to the perception among potential clients, colleagues, and card-carrying OD practitioners themselves of the field as a scattered and inherently lost profession that lacks a core ideology or set of fundamental assumptions.

The most current definition of OD is as follows:

2.46. Definitions of OD

- Orgahisational Development is a planned process of change in an organization's culture through the utilization of behavioral science technologies, research, and theory"(Burke,1982.p.10)
- Organisational Dcvclopment is a long-range effort to improve an organization's problem solving and renewal process, particularly through a more effective and collaborative management of an organization culture with the assistance of a change agent, or catalyst, of and the use of the theory and technology of applied behavioral science, including action research."(French &Bell,1978.p.14)
- Organisational Development is a value-based process of self-assessment and planned changes involving specific strategies and technology,

aimed at improving the overall effectiveness of an organizational system." (Margulies & Raia, 1972.p.24)

- Organisational Development is a planned, behavioral sciences based interventions in work settings for the purpose of improving organizational functioning and individual development." (Porras &Robertson,1992.p.721)
- Organisation Development is a long-term, Planned changes in the culture, technology, and management of a total organization or at least a significant part of the total organization."(Jamieson,Bach kellick, &Kur,1984.p.4)

Organization Development is a planned process of promoting positive humanistically oriented large-system and improvement in organizations through the use of social science theory, action research, and behaviorally based data collection and feedback techniques. Regardless of the definition that one subscribes to, however, it should be apparent when reviewing these definitions that although they differ on several important dimensions, for example, some focus on the importance of technology in the change process, whereas, others explicitly mention top management support, and still others reference values explicitly, they share common components as well.

2.47. A New framework for Organizational Development

Given the variety of issues and complexities regarding the field, there is need to provide a single source, as well as an overarching framework or model, regarding the contemporary practice of OD. Although the framework is relatively self-explanatory, several points should be made about it, first, data represent the central set of inputs (in systems) into the overall process. Data here refers to quantitative, qualitative, or process-based inputs that reflect the different interventions and methodologies. Because many practitioners rely on more than one form of data and in many instances a diagnosis using one method might lead to further examination or an intervention based on another,

Table 1.1. Framework for a driven Organizational Development

<Insert image jpg 2.47.table 1.1Here> no in file

An arrow indicates the reciprocal nature of their relationship. The outcomes of these data-driven methodologies drive the large organizational initiatives, which represent the movement stage in the change process. These initiatives include broad issues such as leadership development, global diversity training, and mission and strategy implementation. Moreover, some of the complexities involved in working with these initiatives as, an OD practitioner include the challenges of using information technology effectively, developing an awareness of diverse cultures and practices in doing OD around the world, and the ethics and values OD practitioners need to embody. These interventions, when pursued in a focused and highly integrated manner, will ultimately help transform the organization and result in improvement and change. In addition, the role of evaluation and linkage research is crucial for establishing the impact and credibility of OD as a field. Although what is important here is the approach and not the outcomes, given the societal importance placed on metrics and numbers, it is time for the field to accept fully its roots in a data- driven approach and understand the value inherent in measuring what we do and how we do it.

2.48. Nature of Organizational Development

Unlike medicine, accounting, law, police work, national politics, and many other disciplines, professions, and vocational callings that one might choose to pursue, all of which have a clear, consistent, and focused sense of purpose, the field of organization development (OD) is somewhat unique in its inherent and fundamental lack of clarity about itself. Organization development is a field that is both constantly evolving and yet constantly struggling with a dilemma regarding its fundamental nature and unique contribution as a collection of organizational scientist and practitioners. (Church, Hurley, & Burke, 1992; Friedlander, 1976, Goodstain, 1984; Greiner, 1980, Sanzgir, & Gottlieb, 1992; Weilbord, 1982) found that OD practitioners have been thinking, writing, and debating about the underlying nature of the field for decades, the field itself has yet come to agreement on its basic boundaries or parameters. Moreover, various practitioner surveys conducted in the 1990s(Church, Burke, & Van Eynde, 1994, Fagenson & Burke, 1990; McMahen & Woodman,1992) have found that the field is no closer to finding the answer to these important questions than it was twenty years ago. (Church, Waclawski, & Siegal, 1996; Jamieson, Bech Kallick, & Kur, 1984; Rothewell, Sullivan &Mclean, 1995) found that it should come as no surprise, then, that one of the most poignant criticisms leveled at OD since its inception is that there are almost as many definitions of the field as there are OD practitioner. (Harvey,1974) posit that the field of OD has been by zealots out to democratize organization. (Churh,2000) posit that there is some disagreement in the field as to what is and is not organizational development.

This lack of unified definition of or approach to the central nature of Organisational Development is due in large part to the diversity of backgrounds of those who engage in Organisational Development practice from forestry, to Law,to history, to the social sciences. Because one of the value of the field is inclusivity, relatively little attention has been paid historically to maintaining boundaries around the practice or labeling of Organisational Development. A cursory review of some of the professional associations with which Organisational Development practitioners, affiliate(see table 1.1), for example, highlight the breadth of membership even among somewhat like-minded groups. Moreover, (Church, Waclawski,&Siegal,1996) found that literally anyone can hang a shingle outside and be a self-proclaimed Organisational Development practitioner. Thus, for some, Organisational Development represents anything and everything that be offered. Moreover, because there are only a handful of Organisational Development doctoral programs in the United States, there is a real sense among many in the field(Allen et al,1993; Church & Burke, 1995; Golembieluski,1989; Van Eynde &Coruzzi, 1993) found that the lack of common education, training, and experience is continuing to damage and erode its overall credibility as a profession. Clearly, given the fractured state of the field and the nature of the many divergent perceptions regarding Organisational Development, there is a need in the literature and with respect to training future practitioners for given the nature of these definitions and collective consulting experience in and exposure to others in the field over the decade. (Church,Burke,&Van Eynde,1994) found that Organisational Development should be conceptualized as representing three essential components.

First and perhaps for foremost, Organisational Development is fundamentally a data-driven process; diagnosis and intervention are based on some form of behaviorally relevant data (such as observations, assessment, and surveys) collected through a process known as action research. Second, the Organisational Development model represents a total system approach to organizational change in which this change is a formal and planned response to targeted organization-wide issues, problems, and challenges. Finally, although this component is controversial and by no means universally accepted as yet, it is strongly believe that values represent a third key component to the field. Organisational Development is (or should be) a normative and humanistic values-based approach to organizational improvement. In short in my own view Organisational

Development work should be focused on and conducted for the good of the individual, as well as the good of the organization. (Church,Waclawski, &Siegal,1996; Margulies &Raio 1990) found that balancing issues of effectiveness and profitability are certainly important for economic success and survival.

2.49. Organizational Development as a Data-Driven Processing Acton Research

(Burke, 1982; French and Bell, 1990) found that one of the most basic notions behind Organisation Development is that change and improvement are conducted through a data-based process known as action research. Kurt Lewin, who first conceptualized action research in 1946 and has often being credited as saying that "there can be no action without research and no research without action "was truly one of the first Scientist-Practitioners in the social sciences and a major contributor to much of the thinking underlying Organisational Development theory and practice. (church, waclawsk, & Burke 2001) found that in Organisational Development work, action research entails systematically gathering data of whatever form, quantitative or qualitative, on the nature of particular problem or situation, analyzing the data to find central themes and patterns, feeding back a summary and analysis of the data in some participative form and then taken action based on what the analysis of the data and resulting diagnosis of the situation suggest. Given this framework, it s easy to see how both the classic and more contemporary Organisational Development tools and techniques described in this paper meet the criterion of being data-driven Organisational Development because they collect and apply information for various problem-solving and improvement purposes. Organization surveys, multisource feedback, focus groups and interviews, personality assessments, process observations and consultation, action learning, appreciative inquiry, and large-scale interventions all fall squarely within this framework. They follow the progression of steps outline in the basic action research approach from data collection, through diagnosis, to taking action for improvement.

The process by which data are used to drive change is a relatively simple one. Lewin, a social psychologist who specialized in studying group dynamics, asserted that individual and organizational transformation is best described as a three-stage process (see figure 1.1)

Figure 1.1. classic change models

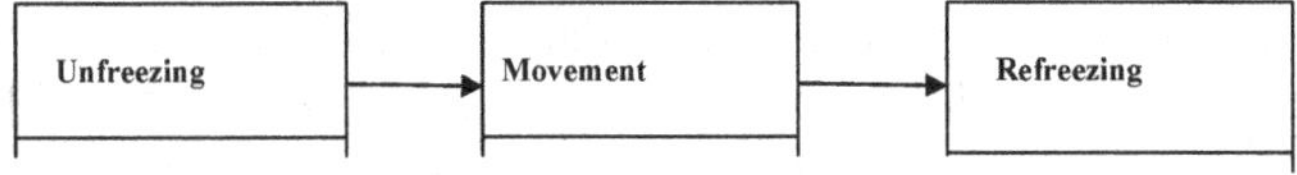

Church, et al,(2001) found that in the **first stage**, unfreezing, the goal is to create motivation or a readiness for change. (Beckhard & Harris, 1987) found that in most cases in OD practice, this translates to surfacing dissatisfaction with the current state and identifying a better or more desirable alternative, which is commonly referred to in OD terms as the ideal or desired future state. An analogy from everyday life is dieting. Most people go on diet because they are unhappy with their weight. It is this dissatisfaction with the current t situation coupled with a vision of a better future state of weighing less and therefore being healthier and looking better, that motivates them to change their eating behavior. The **second stage** in Lewins model, movement, consists of making changes and engaging in new behaviors to help make the desired future state a reality. In short, once the need for a change has been realized, steps towards achieving a new and better state must be taken. In the dieting example, this will represent the point at which the dieter makes a change in behavior – a reduction in caloric intake and an increase in exercise level. In Organisational Development, the movement stage typically translates into focusing ones change efforts at three different levels: individuals, group and organizational. The **third stage**, refreezing, requires establishing a system or process that will solidify (or refreeze) the new desired state.

In the dieting example, this will mean making what people call a permanent lifestyle change, such that the new eating and exercise regimen comes a permanent and normal part of everyday life. In Organisational Development, an example of the refreezing stage would be instilling a new reward and recognition programmed as a result of an organizational culture survey to reinforce a new and desired set of leadership behaviors. (Church, 2006) posit that in reality, the rapid pace of change experienced by most organizations today, refreezing occurs all too infrequently, if at all, and even when it does, it is not likely to last for very long before some other chaotic events affects the organization.

2.51. Organizational Development as a normative process

The third concept, and in many ways the truly unique element, driving Organisational Development theory and practice is the notion that Organisational Development is or at least should be a values-driven, humanistically oriented, normative process for change. (Burke, 1982;Friedlander,1976; Marglilies & Raia 1990) found that Organisational Development is about helping people have better life's at work. Taken by some as an ethical mandate against the perceived evils of organizations, some Organisational Development practitioners focus their efforts on initiatives aimed at improving the state of human dignity, democracy honesty, integrity and empowerment in organizations. (Henry, 1974) posit that these "Organisational Development Missionaries" as they have been called are probably not the norm, they do represent a truly unique aspect to change management. (Roddick, 1994) posit that when certain executives and organizations are heralded for their innovative people oriented practices or cultures, the Organisational Development field is quick to focus on such triumphs of the human spirit at work. (Church & Burke, 1995) found that,one of the results of this emphasis on installing meaning and dignity in the work place (particularly when taken out of context) has been the perception of Organisational Development as been too soft or touchy-feely in focus. Interestingly enough, such perceptions both attract certain types of practitioners and clients while putting off others. (Church & Waclawski

1998) found that the extent to which this values are truly enacted in practice remains a major question for the field, particularly, given the financial realities of a consulting market place where expertise has been devalued and few can afford to stand for professional ideas or integrity, it is none the less important to recognize, appreciate, and even reinforce such values. (Weisboard, 1982) posit that Values derive a profession and make it unique. Clearly, given the moral corruption that exists in some of today's political, social, and organizational systems, its heartening to know that some group of professionals somewhere stands for a higher purpose. (Burke,192; Friedlander, 1976. Gellermann, Frankel & Ladenson, 1990; Goodstein, 1984; Greiner, 1980, Hurley, church Burke, & Van Eynde, 1992, Margulies & Raia 1990) found that the question regarding which values do or should drive the field of Organisational Development has been a topic of debate for decades, and it is strongly believe that Organisational Development does indeed represent a normative approach to organizational change. Just as the fields of industrial organizational (i/o) psychology and human resource development (HRD) are grouped in improving the conditions of people lives and promoting human welfare and learning in organizations, so too is the fields of Oeganisational Development. (Church, Burke, & Van Eynde, 1994) found that not all Organisational Development practitioners act according to such ideas, (Waclawski, Church & Burke, 1995) found that there is a strong bias, and I believe an ethical imperative in Organisational Development work towards promoting human development and positive growth. In sum, Organisational Development driven by a value based, systematic mind-set using action research methods for organizational improvement. Although these three elements represent the basic Hieratical approach taken to

Organisational Development work they do not specifically reflex the role of data in the diagnosis and intervention process itself.

2.52. The role of Data in the Consulting process

(Kolb Frohman, 1970; Nadler, 1977) found that one of the best known approaches to Organisational Development practice is the seven-phase consulting model. Based in Lewin's action research framework, this model consists seven distinct phases that apply to every change initiative or engagement; entry, contracting, data collection, data analysis, data feedback, intervention, and evaluation (See seven-phase of consulting model below).

2.53. Seven-Phase Consulting Model

Phase 1. Entry: initial meeting between client and consultant.The client and consultant meet to explore issues and the possibility of an OD effort. The client assesses 4. The consultant is trustworthy, experiences, and competent. The consultant assesses 4 the client is ready for change and has the resources and power to support change.

Phase 2. Reach agreement on what each will do. This includes determing mutual expectations, expected time frame, schedule of activities, cost of activities and grand rules for proceeding.

Phase 3. Data collection: Gather information about the organization. Interviews, questionnaires, company documents and performance records, focus groups and other methods are used.

Phase 4. Data analysis: Summarize information and draw conclusions. From the data, the client and consultant determine next steps once the diagnosis is understood and accepted.

Phase 5. Data feedback: present summary and conclusions to the client. The consultant presents the summary and the preliminary interpretation, followed by a general discussion to clarify information. Next, the consultant and clients derive at a final diagnosis that accurately describes the organization. Together the generate plans for responding to the issues.

Phase 6. Intervention: Take action. The selected interventions should be a direct reflection and response to the diagnosis.

Phase 7. Evaluation: determines success or failure. Change efforts are evaluated to see if the desired change has occurred. In general, the seven phase model has a wide range of application in a varity of consulting situations and is especially important for OD practitioners for three reasons:

- It reinforce the centrality of data in the process of organization development and change
- Shows how and when data should be used to inform OD practice, and
- Is based on a system approach to organizations

Phase I, entry, represent the first meeting between 5 he OD Practitioner and Client. (Katz & Kahn, 1987) found that the practitioners first exposure to the current client system) is critical in terms of building what we might call a facilitative (as opposed to expert) relationship. Typically, during this initial meeting, both the client and the OD consultant are assessing one another, to determine whether they will be able to collaborate on the pending change initiative. This process includes the potential clients attempts to determine the competency and the experience level of the OD practitioner, as well as the practitioner's initial assessment of the presenting problem(that is the symptom) and it's underlying causes(the real problem), which will need to be examine through some form of data collection. As the potential client looks for signs of report with the practitioner, the practitioner looks for the signs of the potential clients true level of motivation for and commitment to the potential change effort. The fact is that, if a client has neither the intention for the resources to implement a significant change effort, there is little reason from an OD perspective to pursue the situation in this context. In short, the quality of the interaction here determines whether the OD effort will occur at all, if positive relations are not established, the relationship and thus the change effort will go no further or still in mid process.(Block,1981;Burke,1994) found that contracting, **Phase 2** , consists of setting the expectations, role, and anticipated outcomes for the change effort. (Church,&Waclawski,1998) found that from an Organisational Development perspective, the preferred mode here is to rely on open and honest communication rather than on a more formerlized legal contracting process, though the latter is often requested in today's litigious and increasingly vendor-driven business environment. For example, if a client is interested in undertaking a series of one-on-one interviews to help diagnose the functioning of the senior leadership team of the organization, he or she may call in an external or internal Organisational Development practitioner to do this work. During entry and contracting, the consultant and client will not only discuss the work to be done and the practitioner's qualifications for doing this work, but they will also explore interpersonal issues(such as whether the two can communicate and therefore work with one another) and what can and cannot be realistically accomplished as a result of the diagnostic interviews and feedback process.

Once entry, and contracting have been successfully completed, the internal or external Organisational Development consultant will need to collect data about the organization in order to gain a better understanding of the problems to be solved or the underlying issues at hand . To this end, **Phase 3 through 5** of the consulting model concerns the collection, analysis, and feedback data. These data can either be quantitative (multisource feedback, survey instruments, personality assessments, or performance measures) or qualitative (observations, interviews, and focus groups, or process measures) in nature, or some combination of both. The consultant at this point will begin collecting and analyzing the major themes in interview data. By gathering perceptual, attitudinal, and perhaps behaviorally based critical incident data through one-on-one discussions, the practitioner is positioning himself or herself to develop a detailed understanding about the nature of the team's functioning. Moreover, by directing the discussion as toward a focus on the nature of the team dynamics now, where members want these to be, , real or and what barriers, real or perceived, might exist, the challenges but also simultaneously creating energy for change on the part of team members. This energy, caused by attending to the perceptual gap between the existing and future states, is one of the basic means for initiating behavior change in the Lewinian approach.Once data have been collected and analyzed, **phase 6** can begin: specific interventions base on the diagnostic summary performed using the interview results can be interactively discussed and selected for subsequent action. The important point to remember here is that regardless of which interventions are chosen, their determination should be based on an interpretation of the issues inherent in the data itself(and not simply because it is the trendiest, most expensive, or most flashy OD, I/O, or HRD technique available), and jointly selected by the consultant and client. This leads to commitment on the part of the client and ultimately contributes to the success of the entire change process.

Finally, an evaluation of the success of the OD effort should always be undertaken. Often this require collecting additional data regarding the impact of the intervention in the light of the deliverables that were agreed on in the contracting phase, as well as brainstorming about process improvements for future OD efforts. Clearly this is easier said than done. (Golembiewski &Sun, 1990, Porras & R obertson, 1992; Woodman & Wayne,1983) found that one of the truly unfortunate situations in many OD efforts over the past thirty years and one that has damaged the reputation of the field, somewhat as well, has been the lack of significant attention to evaluating the success or failure of an OD process. As many researchers and OD scholars have noted, there is a real need in the field for the consistent application of evaluation strategies to the entire consulting cycle. Although some firms believe in the value-driven approach enough to forgo this element, it is not a helpful or a recommended approach to practice. Overall, the internal and external practice of OD work is truly data-driven approach to helping organizations identify specific problems and issues and plan for improvement.

2.54. Application of OD Initiative in Bankers Institute of Rural Development (BIRD)

The initiative for Organisational Development programs comes from an organization that has a problem. This means that top management or someone authorized by top management is aware that a problem exists and has decided to seek help in solving it. There is a direct analogy here to the practice of psychotherapy: The client or patient must actively seek help in finding a solution to his problems. This indicates a willingness on the part of the client organization to accept help and assures the organization that management is actively concerned. (Burke, 1994) posit that Organization Development is a planned process of change in an organization's culture through the utilization of behavioral science technologies, research, and theory. (Cummings and Worley, 1993)found that OD is "a system wide application of behavioral science knowledge to the planned development and reinforcement of organizational strategies, structures and processes for improving an organization's effectiveness " As the above definitions suggest O.D. is a planned and sustained process of change to improve organizational effectiveness. Its target of change is the total organization or system. It applies the knowledge, insights, tools and techniques of applied behavioral sciences. Organization Development as a strategy of change with employee participation is being practiced world over in various organizations. There is a proliferation of O.D. approaches as different approaches are found succeeding in different organizations and environments. The present paper aims at sharingthe experience of Bankers Institute of Rural Development (BIRD) in conducting an Organization Development Initiative-a novel O.D. Intervention for this population-in 49 Regional Rural Banks (RRBs) in India during 1994-97.

2.55. The Background of the O.D. Initiative in the RRBs

The RRBs are a set of state-sponsored rural banks in India, each covering one or two districts with the mandate to provide banking facilities to rural clientele engaged in agriculture and non-farm activities. They have proved to be most appropriate grass root rural credit institutions in India on account of their wide branch network in remote unbanked areas, small size, local feel and rural orientation. Although, these banks had served well in providing various types of financial services to the rural customers, especially mobilizing small, rural savings and extending credit support to state sponsored poverty alleviation programmes, they suffered from several handicaps, like, poor recovery of loans, low level of business, undue restrictions on their business operations (e.g., they were required to lend only to the poor clients at concessional rates of interest). Most of these banks incurred continuous losses due to thin/negative financial margin, poor recoveries and high establishment costs in relation to their volume of business. Particularly, under the government-sponsored programmes, the RRBs had been left with very little choice of customers based on banking considerations. This was more on account of the way the sponsored programmes were actually implemented under external pressures and interference than the manner in which these programmes were originally designed. Over the years, the staff of these banks developed a complacent attitude about profit and business, apathy towards the customers and a deceptive self-assurance about the future of their organization, the attitude commonly observed in public sector organizations. During early 90s, with a view to containing the sagging performance of the economy, an era of economic liberalization had to be ushered in by Government of India, which focused on economic growth through deregulation and market orientation. The reforms also touched the banking sector with emphasis on revamping the banking institutions into organizationally strong, vibrant and self-sustaining systems. Several policy measures were introduced to lift the restrictions on lending rates, choice of clientele, investment opportunities, location of branches, etc., in order to improve RRBs' efficiency, productivity, profitability and long term sustainability. In this context, the RRBs needed to change their business outlook, become more responsive to customer needs, reengineer their systems and procedures and, above all, reorient the mind-set of their employees. The reform package took care of introducing an enabling policy environment by lifting unnecessary curbs on RRBs operations. It also included preparation of long range, bank-specific business development plans (i.e.Development Action Plans (DAPs) taking into account the bank's strengths, weaknesses, opportunities and threats. Based on some broad guidelines issued by National Bank for Agriculture and Rural Development (NABARD), the Development Financial Institution (DFI) for rural sector in the country, each RRB was advised to prepare its own Development Action Plan. The Government also took care to inject fresh capital to cleanse RRBs' balance sheets. Emphasis was put on strengthening the human resources in these organizations through proper training. Initially, the RRB employees did not accept the DAPs as they were not involved in its preparation and suspected that it implied additional workload on them without any scope for personal growth or benefits as mostly the plans tended to be and were perceived as a top down process. They looked upon DAPs as "instruments of exploitation" and "another experiment with RRBs." Bankers Institute of Rural Development (BIRD) had long experience of training the RRB staff and was familiar with their problems and their general mind set. Based on interactions with BIRD in various forums where revamping of RRBs was discussed, it was increasingly realized by policy framers that a kind of intervention like O.D.and not merely training in banking skills, was needed for the RRBs. At the instance of NABARD and Reserve

Bank of India (RBI), BIRD took up the responsibility of designing an appropriate O.D. intervention in RRBs selected for revamping in the first phase. The O.D. approaches were suitably modified through intensive faculty deliberations to design an intervention package named the Organization Development Initiative for these banks. Since the O.D. Initiative had to be done in a large number of RRBs (49) in a short spar of one year, the intervention was to be of short duration and a large number of Faculty Members from BIRD and its 4 sister training institutes (i.e., the National Bank Staff College, College of Agricultural Banking and 2 Regional Training Colleges of NABARD) had to be pressed into service to complete the job in time. Thus, it was an intervention by Faculty Consultants as a part of the reform package. The consultants were not invited by the RRBs themselves but by their majority stakeholders (i.e., the Government of India) and the policy makers like Reserve Bank of India (RBI)-the Central Bank of the country-and National Bank for Agriculture and Rural Development (NABARD)-the Apex Rural Development Bank to initiate this HRD intervention.

2.56. Objectives of the O.D. Initiative

Normally, O.D. objectives are set by the client organization. Contrary to this, in the present case, the objectives of O.D. Initiative were evolved by BIRD at the instance of and through a dialogue with the majority stakeholders of RRBs (i.e., the Government of India) and the controlling agencies (i.e., RBI and NABARD) and reflected their concern to make the RRBs efficient and viable organizations. More specifically, the intervention was aimed at:

- Sensitizing RRB employees to appreciate the new realities in the context of reforms in the banking sector.
- Developing among them a sense of belonging to their organization Integrating their personal goals with Organizational goals
- Building confidence and belief in their own capabilities to shoulder higher responsibilities.
- Enabling them to internalize and own up to their problems
- Developing problem solving abilities among them
- Developing collaborative attitude and team spirit among them.
- Building a climate of trust, openness, and free communication in RRBs

In brief, the task was to find an appropriate intervention strategy enabling the RRBs' human resources to halt organizational decay and create conditions for organizational renewal.

2.57. About BIRD

BIRD is India's apex training institute in rural development banking, promoted and substantially funded by NABARD. It is an autonomous body with mandate covering training, research and consultancy in areas of rural development and rural development banking. The Institute enjoys an excellent reputation in the country's banking circles. Through long association with RRBs as a training institute, BIRD had developed a special relationship with the RRB system combining in-depth knowledge about the RRBs and an understanding of the psyche of the RRB employees. The high credibility of BIRD among RRBs had given it a unique advantage to act as trustworthy consultants and counselors to RRBs. This helped acceptability of BIRD's Faculty Members as O.D. facilitators in RRBs.

2.58. Philosophical Underpinnings of the O.D. Initiative :

The O.D. Initiative designed by BIRD borrowed several principles from applied behavioral sciences, adult learning, action research and T-Group learning. Some of the assumptions of the design were the following:

- People have a positive direction and can make contribution to the organization, if they are allowed to participate in the planning and the decision making process.
- The best way to bring change in organizations is to empower the employees through entrusting them with responsibility and giving positive feedback for initiative, risk taking, creativity and good performance.
- Groups are the basic organizational building blocks and peer pressure is the most powerful impetus for change.
- Change can be brought by building empowered teams in the organizations through team building efforts.
- In most organizations, the level of inter-personal support, trust and cooperation is lower than desirable and necessary.
- Organizations are inter-related systems and change, in order to be sustainable, has to cover all subsystems.

- Organizational functioning is enhanced when people feel comfortable expressing both their opinions and feelings.
- Hence conflicts that are expressed and addressed openly can be helpful in bringing about change.
- There is a need for an outside facilitator having expertise in process facilitation to initiate the O.D. intervention.

2.59. Design criteria of the Organisational Development. Initiative

The Organisational Development. Initiative was designed by BIRD and it sister training institutes incorporating the above principles. The design criteria established were:

- The process should insist on complete involvement and participation of a large cross section of employees from all levels and pressure groups.
- It should encourage the participants to think and analyze and sort out the problems themselves.
- The facilitator will not provide any training inputs or prescriptions to solve the bank's problems
- Through the process of brainstorming, the employees will find answers to the problems identified by them as critical.
- O.D. interventions were to be carried out in the bank's own premises, with minimum dislocation of the normal schedule.

2.60. Expected Results

At the end of the O.D. Initiative program, the RRB employees were expected to do the following:

- Communicate more openly
- Collaborate more effectively
- Take more responsibility
- Share a common vision for the organization
- Solve problems more effectively
- Show more respect and support for others
- Interact with each other more effectively
- Be more open to experimentation and new ways of doing things
- Be more prepared for change
- Actively participate in planning and decision making
- Promote free flow of information
- Function strategically rather than simply in response to stimulus

It was expected that the above developments will help to create a healthy work culture in RRBs, increase employee satisfaction and, thereby, lead to higher productivity and profitability.

2.61. Methodology

The methodology adopted had the following components:

Sensitization of the Chairmen and General Managers of selected RRBs to the concepts of O.D. and group dynamics prior to O.D. intervention and enlisting their support to O.D. process

Intervention at the bank's own environment involving a large cross section of employees and senior executives.

Creating a climate and setting in which hierarchies are broken to facilitate frank and open discussions Brainstorming and group process to identify bank's problems and to find solutions thereto by examining all possible alternatives. Analysis of bank's performance data and its comparison with other banks, and examination of the replicability of success stories and best practices followed by other RRBs

2.62. Outcomes

The outcome of this process were:

- Building a Mission statement, Vision and Goals Formulation of strategies and workable action plans for achieving the goals.
- Exhaustive debate on various issues for diagnosing the organization's problems and arriving at consensus on the strategies and Action Plans.
- Presentation of the Action Plans to the Bank's Board seeking its support.
- Identification of internal Facilitators to take the O.D. Initiative message to other staff (who did not participate in the process) and sustaining the tempo generated by the initiative.
- Conducting studies and research on the RRBs Restructuring and giving feedback to policy makers for suitable policy correction.
- Organizing seminars/workshops to disseminate BIRD's experience in conducting the O.D. Initiative and insights gained and to facilitate wider debate on the subject.

2.63.0. Organisational Development. Initiative Program Modules

2.63.1. The Organisational Development. Initiative design consisted of four modules:

- A four day sensitization program for the Chairmen/General Managers of selected RRBs at BIRD prior to actual O.D. intervention in individual banks
- A five day on-location O.D. program at the Bank's Head Office
- A two day sensitization program for selected Branch Managers at RRB Head Office
- A meeting with the Board of Directors at the end of the on-location program

2.64.0. Organisational Development. Initiative Process

The process intervention by faculty consultants in the second and third module are discussed in detail in the following paragraphs:

2.64.1. Organisational Development. Intervention Program at the Bank's Head Office

A five-day program was conducted at the Head Office of the Bank in which all departmental heads participated besides the Chairman, General Manager, a few Branch Managers and representatives of the Unions and various pressure groups. The total number of participants was kept within 30. The seating arrangement was circular suggesting equality of status of all participants. Each one was required to wear a name badge. The module started with the Chairman explaining the objectives of the meeting and inviting the participants to participate freely without any fear or inhibition. This was followed by a brief presentation by the Faculty indicating the present position of the bank and how it compared with other banks, backed by analysis of data. The purpose was "to showy them the mirror" and sensitize them to their present position. The following norms of brain storming and discussions were laid down:

- All will participate as equals.
- Any idea from the participants, however wild, will be welcome.
- No one will attack an idea, but one was free to enrich it.
- Constraints should not be quoted to justify why something was not possible, rather one should suggest what could be possible in spite of constraints.
- There should not be any personal attacks.

The discussions opened with the participants' reaction on the present status of the bank. Since this was the first ever occasion when the staff shared the platform with the Chairman and other senior members of the management to discuss the banks' problems, a lot of suppressed anger against past injustices were expressed, anomalies and inequities in the present set up pointed out and the rationale of the reforms were questioned. The Chairman and the General Manager were briefed earlier not to react but to listen patiently. This helped tempers to cool down making the participants receptive and ready to actively participate in the proceedings. The participants were asked to ponder over the following questions:

- What would you like your bank to become in the next 2 to 3 years?
- What, in your opinion, are the critical areas which require priority/attention to achieve the above goals?
- Answers to these questions facilitated a process of joint diagnosis of the problems and goal setting. Thereafter, the participants were encouraged to identify key performance areas and formulate strategies for organizational growth and effectiveness based on Strengths, Weaknesses, Opportunities and Threats (SWOT) analysis. After this, the process of action planning for accomplishing the goals were chalked out through group process, first in small groups and then discussing them in large groups. During the process of action planning, the RRBs staff also identified the support needed to execute the action plans in terms of new systems and procedures, HRD support and policy changes, etc. While preparing the Action Plans for each functional area, the participants were encouraged to addressed the following questions:
- What is to be done?
- How is this to be done?
- Who will do it?
- What changes in systems and procedures will be necessary?
- How progress will be monitored?

- The Faculty Consultants joined the discussions and presented a range of alternative solutions by quoting best practices in other banks, whenever there was a stalemate in the discussions. The suggestions were made not as prescriptions, but as a means of enlarging the perspectives of the participants and helping them to choose from several alternatives after weighing their relative merits. The strategies which emerged covered all important areas like deposits, advances, recovery, investments, housekeeping, customer service, systems and procedures, image building and human resource development, etc. At the end of the program, there was a high level of enthusiasm, commitment to implement the action plans and a sense of achievement and optimism about the bank's future.

2.65. Organisational Development. Intervention Program for Branch Managers of RRBs

A two-day sensitization program for selected Branch Managers was conducted at Head office immediately after the program for Head Office officials. A similar process of objective setting by the Chairman, briefing by the Faculty Consultants, and norms setting was followed before starting the debate. The Branch Managers also took the opportunity to express their feelings of neglect by the Head Office, highlighted the problems faced by them in the field and the areas in which they would expect Head Office support.

2.66. The Branch Managers were then asked to respond to two questions:

- What, as a Branch Manager, can you do on your own without any assistance from the Head Office?
- What more can you do with Head Office assistance?
- Answers to these questions in a group drove home the point that the Branch Managers, indeed, had a large operating space of their own. They could do many things and achieve significant business results without any support from Head Office. By examples and anecdotes from other banks discussions were held on positive changes that pro-active Branch Managers could bring about in their branches. The Branch Managers were then divided into 2 to 3 groups to discuss the strategy to be adopted in key operational areas and answer similar questions (e.g., "What is to be done?"). The group presentation of the strategy was further discussed in the larger group to finalize the Action Plans for each key operational area (deposit, advances, recoveries, image building, etc.) The new points in the Branch Managers' Action Plans were dovetailed into the Action Plans of Head Office officials to finalize the Strategic Action Plans for the bank as a whole. The finalized Action Plans were presented to the Board of Directors of the bank the next day in a special meeting convened for the purpose. With this the O.D. Intervention came to an end.

2.67. Follow-up

The facilitators visited the bank again after a gap of six months to one year to make an assessment of the changes observed in the bank both in business parameters and organizational processes. While the data on the business parameters were collected from bank's records, the data on organizational processes were collected by interviews, group meetings and process observations. The findings and observations of the consultants were shared with the Chairman and the Board, highlighting in the areas which needed their special attention.

2.68. The Impact of the O.D. Initiative

Evaluating the impact of O.D. is always a difficult task. There is no consensus yet among the O.D. specialists as to the most appropriate method or approach for evaluation of O.D. BIRD has so far not done any scientific evaluation of the impact of its O.D. Initiative in RRBs. Assessments have, however, been made based on the feedback received from the banks themselves, their own impressions about changes after the O.D. Initiative, and recorded observations by the Faculty consultants during their subsequent visits to the banks. There has been no comparison between the "control" and "experimental" groups of RRBs to establish that the RRBs involved in the O.D. Initiative fared better than those not involved. Similarly, in the absence of any bench marking prior to the intervention, it has not been possible to prove by research that improvement process has quickened after O.D. intervention. So, the assessment so far made is, at best, impressionistic. A mid-term evaluation of 20 RRBs with O.D. intervention based on their published data for periods of 3 to 4 years showed that 14 of them have achieved sizable increase in their business levels, per employee business, improvement in recovery of loans, increase in financial margins, improvement in profitability, overall improvement in systems and procedure, customer service and image, etc., after O.D. intervention. But the change could not be attributed to the O.D. Initiative alone. A conjunction of several factors, like policy changes, initiative by the Chairman and the staff, support from other stake holders, etc., could have contributed to the result. Organizations are very "noisy" environments. That is, at any given time, many changes, planned or unplanned, may be taking place. It is, therefore, not possible to isolate the contribution of any single factor to the ultimate outcome (Walters, 1990). In fact, during process of O.D. Initiative in the 49 selected RRBs, a number of developments, both favorable and unfavorable to revamping, took place. Among the favorable factors were (a) enabling policy changes removing several restrictions on RRBs as regards the clientele, interest rates, investments, etc., (b) capital injection, (c) close monitoring of the progress by policy makers. Among the unfavorable factors were (a) rejection of the demand from RRBs for continued parity in pay scales with Commercial banks in the subsequent pay revision after initially allowing such parity since September 1987 and (b) considerable delay in payment of arrears of earlier pay revision to RRB employees. It is, therefore, impossible to isolate the contribution of the O.D. Initiative, or for that matter any single factor, in improvement of the "outcome variables." The O.D. Initiative could have been a catalyst in expediting the change, but it is difficult to say to what extent. Similarly, the RRBs showed encouraging improvement in "process variables." There was greater communication sharing, more delegation of powers to lower levels, more visible sense of belonging among staff, more willingness to take responsibilities, more participation in planning and decision making, a greater sense of achievement and empowerment among the RRB staff. Though these conclusions are not research based, there are ample reports from the banks that the O.D. Initiative has made a noticeable impact in improving the organizational climate in their banks.

Further, there has been a spate of demands from these banks for fresh doses of the O.D. Initiative and similar requests from other banks not covered under the O.D. Initiative for similar intervention. These lend substance to the "felt satisfaction" that the O.D. Initiative did have a positive impact in the RRBs.

2.69.0. Comparison of BIRD's O.D. Initiative Module with the Conventional Organisational Development. Interventions

2.69.1. Points of similarity.

BIRD's O.D. Initiative seeks to bring change in the entire organization:

- Mission, strategy, systems, culture, climate and employees.
- Ensures Chief Executive Officers' commitment and support to the intervention.
- BIRD's O.D. Initiative aims at both commitment and capacity building of the employees by providing clarifications and hints at the flaws in the existing systems and procedures
- Involves employees' participation at all levels in planning and implementing change
- Intervention is by outside facilitators Brainstorming among staff to diagnose

the problems of the organization and find solutions

- Provides a forum to air long standing grievances; helps in catharsis.
- Showing of the mirror by O.D. facilitators to bring home the point to the employees of the real state of affairs in the organization
- SWOT analysis of the organization by the employees and building strategy, capitalizing on strengths and opportunities and attacking weaknesses and threats
- No prescription by the O.D. facilitators to solve the organizations' problems-solutions are found by the employees themselves

2.70. Consensus building at all levels of the organization on the organizations' Mission and Strategy

Practicing new behavior to build the desired climate of openness, trust, freedom of expression, tolerance of others' opinions, appreciation of good work, working as a team, ownership of problems and discovery of a sense of power to solve problems while working in groups.In brief, efforts are focused to increase self control and self direction for the people within the organization.

2.71. How this initiative is different from conventional Organisational Development.

BIRD's Organisational Development. Initiative was taken up at a large number of organizations at a time by BIRD and its sister Institutes. The intervention was by professional trainers without having any Organisational Development. experience but having intimate knowledge of the organizations in question and their employees. The consultants were not engaged by the clients (viz., the organizations themselves), but by major stakeholders-the Government of India implementing revamping package for such organizations. The Organisational Development. intervention was a part of the revamping package for RRBs under Banking Sector Reforms. It was of a short duration, the first intervention lasting about 10 days and the follow-up visit for 5 to 6 days after a gap of 6 months to one year. Only a fraction of the organizations' employees were exposed to the process. Some internal facilitators were trained in the Organisational Development. facilitation techniques to carry on the message to other staff/branches. Outside consultants were engaged to keep in touch with the banks due to other pressing engagements of Organisational Development. facilitators. They made independent assessment of the impact of the Organisational Development. Initiative and identified areas which required further support. New training programmes were designed and delivered by BIRD based on training needs identified during the Organisational Development. Initiative and follow up visits in order to build the skill and competence of RRB staff in critical areas.

2.72. Lessons Learned

Organizing the Organisational Development. Initiative in several grassroots institutions at a time by a team of dedicated Faculty Members was a Herculean task, but it gave the faculty an immense opportunity to practice counseling skills and enrich their understanding of the interpersonal dynamics at work. Designing and conducting Organisational Development. intervention at such a massive scale was itself quite challenging. It was gratifying to know that the module worked effectively in totally different situations and contexts. There was initial resistance in some banks to the Organisational Development. process from the top executives and the employees but in the end there was great enthusiasm among the staff to accept and participate in the change process. Certain limitations have also come to our notice in the design and delivery of Organisational Devlopment. intervention: There was slow down of the euphoria in most of the banks one or two months after the Organisational Development. intervention. Since the gap between the first and second contact was long, the tempo could not be sustained in many banks. Hence, a need was felt for more frequent contacts with banks by engaging outside consultants. The follow-up of the Organisational Development. Initiative by the banks themselves was not uniform. The banks which took interest to spread the message to other staff through internal facilitators did better as compared to banks which did not follow up adequately. Though BIRD had organized special programmes for the internal facilitators to equip them with some Organisational Development. Initiative facilitation skills, their effectiveness was limited due to their low acceptability among the employees. The banks where the Chairmen actively supported the Organisational Development. Initiative process and implemented action plans fared better than the banks where such active support was lacking. In some banks where the Chairman changed after the Organisational Development. intervention, the new incumbents did not show much enthusiasm for implementing the action plans. It was realized that Organisational Development. Initiative alone cannot bring desired changes in the organization without supporting policy environment and commitment/support from other players. The Organisational Development. Initiative also raised hopes among the employees for better incentives and rewards along with the optimism and positive outlook it generated. It was, therefore, felt necessary to support the expectations of the employees with some positive incentives/ rewards.

2.73. Organizational Development as a tool system approach to change

(Katz Kahn, 1978) posit that Organisational Development is fundamentally grounded in a social systems approach. From this perspective, such as people, technology, or processes, that operates as a collective entity in response to changes in and pressures from the external environment, such as competitions, customers, or government regulations. An example from biology is that of a single cell existing within a large organism. In this context, the organization, is the cell, and the larger organism is the global business environment. The cell, although self-contained with its own series of inputs and outputs, depends on the larger organism to survive. The larger organism, in turn is dependent on the functioning of the unique cells comprising it because these cell collectively transform and produce materials that the vital to the organism's existence. As part of its function, the cell inputs certain materials from the larger organism, transforms them into the organism for use by other cells. Thus, the individual cell and the large organism form a symbolic relationship, each is dependent on the other for survival and growth by applying systems theory, an organization is seen as operating in much the same way, it takes in inputs from the outside world; such as raw materials, intellectual capital, human resources, or money for goods and services, and acts on them to transform them into new products or services and then export them back into the business environment for distribution and disposal(see figure 1.2.). (Burke &Litwin, 1992) found that large-scale OD and change efforts are seen as occurring within an organizational system and are generally initiated in response to changes in the business or external environment in which the organization operates.

Figure 1.2.Systems Approach Model

<Insert image **jpg 2.73.figure 1.2Here> no in file**

Given this framework, it is apparent that an OD model is somewhat different from other consulting approaches because most OD interventions used are aimed at changing the entire system, as opposed to a specific portion or segment of the organization.

2.74. Functions of Organisational Development

(Burke,1994;Block, 1981) found that much of the trade literature and case studies regarding the practice of Organisational Development focus on the skills, challenges, and role of external consultants ,and indeed for many this lifestyle represents the perceptually more clamoring choice.(Van Enynde, Church, & Burke, 1994) found that at least, half of all practitioners in the Organisational Development, Human Resources Development, and even Industrial Organisational psychology arenas work internally in corporations, universities and nonprofit organizations, unfortunately, (Mcmahan & Woodman, 1992) found that this role and consequently the contribution of this half is underemphasized, underrepresented and in some cases under appreciated in the field. (Church, & Mcmahan, 1996; mcmahan, & Woodman,1992) found that despite some popular with the fortune 500 industries and the fortune 100 fastest growing firms has shown that the primary client in most internal Organisational Development efforts is senior management. Perhaps this is not surprising given that senior leadership support is almost always as a necessity for an effective intervention or systemic initiative,(Church,2000) posit that this reinforces the notion that internal Organisational Development practitioners must be skilled at working within the political and cultural landscape of the organization if they are to effect change from within. Despite an apparent resurgent interest in the field, the state of the Organisational Development function in the mid-1990s was less than optimal. Survey results by (Church,& Mcmahan, 1996, Golembiewski 1989) found that only 34, percent and 26 percent of the fortune fastest growing firms and industries, respectively, had "Well established" functions, with the rest of the responses scattered among such categories as struggling(respectively,20 percent and 18 percent), worried(7 percent and 5 percent), or even nonexistent(9, percent and 3 percent),furthermore in some organizations, the term OD has such negative connections(as being ineffective or too "touching feeling") that alternative terms such as organizational effectiveness have been created. In other organizations, this manifests itself as more of an issue of the location of OD within other groups, such as HRD, personnel research, or even the occasional organizational learning function. (Church, Waclawski, Mc Hennry, & Mckenna, 1998) found that at Microsoft, for example, some of the more strategic-level OD efforts are conducted through the executive and management development function. Although it is likely given the improvement in the global economy in that past few years that internal OD functions have started to become more prominent once again (and particularly in responses to the changing nature of work and emerging trends in training and retention issues among younger workers), it remains an unfortunate reality that many organizations either place little emphasis on or do not have internal OD function at their disposal at all. (Church & Waclawski,1998) found that it is important to reorganize that most of the leg work of organizational change and improvement is driven by these internal practitioners. As a field, we need to begin to reorganize these individuals more (and conversely, not chastise them for having "sold out" to big business).This means more partnerships (rather than circumnavigation) and more shared learning and skills across the internal-external boundary, from the internal side, this also means focusing more on collaborating with externals as opposed to focusing on issues of turf, and less application of the vendor mind- self to the way external work is contracted and used, before the unique contribution of the entire field has been eroded or supplanted by other consulting models. In short, we need to leverage our strengths as a field of internal and external practitioners to help promote OD and improve the state of organizations.

2.75. Characteristics of Organisational Development

Long term plan: It is planned and long-term–the process is based on gathering data and planned with the expectation of changes taking years.

Change: OD is a planned strategy to bring about organizational change. The change effort aims at specific objectives and is based on a diagnosis of problem areas.

Change Agent: It involves change agent–there is a distinct role for an active facilitator and ombudsmen of the process, to ensure that changes are real; he stimulate, facilitate, and coordinate change.

Action oriented: It's action-oriented–instead of being descriptive of necessary changes, organizational development is diagnostic and prescriptive, seeking measurable results.

Collaborative: OD is typically involves a collaborative approach to change that includes involvement and participation of the organization members most affected by the changes

Performance: OD programs include an emphasis on ways to improve and enhance performance and quality.

Learning: It involves learning principles–individuals, groups and managers at all levels of the organization must re-learn how to function together. Managers who embrace organizational development must be committed to effecting fundamental changes in the organization. The learners' experiences in the training environment should be the kind of human problems they encounter at work. The training should NOT be all theory and lecture.

Systems orientation: OD represents a system approach concerned with the interrelationship of divisions, departments, groups, and individuals as interdependent subsystems of the total organization, must work together.

Scientific: OD is based upon scientific approaches to increase organization effectiveness.

Humanistic Values: Positive beliefs about the potential of employees.

Problem Solving: It is problem-oriented–a multidisciplinary approach is taken to apply theory and research to effect solutions; problems are identified, data is gathered, corrective action is taken, progress is assessed, and adjustments in the problem solving process are made as needed. This process is known as Action Research.

Contingency Orientation: Actions are selected and adapted to fit the need.

Levels of Interventions: Problems can occur at one or more level in the organization so the strategy will require one or more interventions.

2.76. Organisational Development: it's relevance to Holiness Power Bible Ministries

Organisational Development will help to improve "Holiness Power Bible Ministries" capacity to handle its internal and external functioning and relationships. This would include such things as improved interpersonal and group processes, more effective communication, enhanced ability to cope with ministries problems of all kinds, more effective decision processes, more appropriate leadership style, improved skill in dealing with destructive conflict, and higher levels of trust and cooperation among organizational members. Holiness power Bible Church since inception has encountered so many problems. Apart from the sudden decline in the church attendance and worship, Capacity building is another contending problem faced by Holiness Power Bible Church and other non-profit organisationns as they rely on external funding such as: government funds, grants from charitable foundations, direct donations, to maintain their operations, though Holiness Power Bible Church as a new Church (just 6years old) maintain its operations through donations by members and tithes and offering and special contributions from which the church create programs, hire and maintain full-time workers, sustain facilities, and maintain tax-exempt status. Perhaps, this might be the reasons why the church is finding it very difficult to meet up its financial obligations. Another problem spotted out is the GO's "Utterances and his unfavorable, "Rules and Regulations of the church" which has a tremendous effects on the poor church attendance, relationship with members, church finances and programs. Secular management development educators have long been well aware of how leader assumptions about human nature influence educational processes and outcomes. One of most popular and enduring theories in this vein is McGregor's (1960) Theory X & Y model of these assumptions. Theory X assumes that: people dislike putting forth effort; they try to avoid responsibility; they prefer to be told what to do; and must be coerced and controlled to achieve goals. Theory Y, on the other hand, assumes, among other things, that: putting forth effort is natural; people can learn to be responsible and self-directed; and that they will be intrinsically motivated to achieve goals they believe in or are committed to. Theory Y views the symptoms associated with Theory X as caused by the institutional environment. "If employees are lazy, indifferent, unwilling to take responsibility, intransigent, uncreative, uncooperative, Theory Y implies that the causes lie in management's methods of organization and control" (p. 48). Weisbord (1987) posited that all people have a combination of both X and Y tendencies. Which of these is more dominant in their behavior depends on which inclinations the milieu of organizational structures and managerial practices promotes and reinforces. Balfour and Marini (1991) found that the Theory X perspective has led to organizational structures and educational processes which treat adults as children. In the Holiness Power Bible Church this is apparent where, "for the good of the church members," pressure exists, either implicitly or explicitly, to conform to externally imposed, often extrabiblical behavioral norms and doctrinal standards. When pastors and leaders tell people what is right or wrong, what to do or not to do, and what the Bible really says, it is no wonder that people grow passive, lethargic, and irresponsible. (Sievers, 1994) posit that when leaders work from a Theory X perspective, they develop organizations and processes which perpetuate immaturity, thus dependency, in followers. A Theory X church environment reinforces Theory X attitudes and behaviors in church members. Balfour and Marini propose as a counterbalance a Theory Y approach to adult education which recognizes the relative independence, larger experience base, and more mature cognitive capacity of the adult learner. These distinctions roughly parallel and are largely derived from Knowles' (1978) philosophy of andragogy, (Franklin & Freeland, 1989) found that effective pastor's and trainers hold Theory Y assumptions and are more likely to create collaborative learning environments for their members. The Christian corollary of Theory Y education recognizes that the average Christian adult, with the proper tools and a conducive learning environment, is as capable as any theologian of learning spiritual truth and developing righteous behavioral habits through his/her own meditation, study, and practice. The OD objectives stem from a value system based on an optimistic view of the nature of man — that man in a supportive environment is capable of achieving higher levels of development and accomplishment which is in line with the Theory Y assumption.

Formula (D x V x F>R) of David Gleicher(3,4) is used to decide if Holiness Power Bible Church is ready for change.

Where Dx =Dissatisfaction with the present situation

Vx =A vision of what is possible in the future

F =Achievable first step towards reaching this vision.

R =Resistance to Change

Dissatisfaction x Vision x First Steps > Resistance to Change

According to David Gleicher three components must all be present to overcome the resistance to change in Holiness Power Bible Church: Dissatisfaction with the present situation, a vision of what is possible in the future, and achievable first steps towards reaching this vision. According to him if any of the three is zero or near zero, the product will also be zero or near zero and the resistance to change will dominate which has been the case of the church and hence the need for Organisational Development in Holiness power

Bible Ministries. This model is use for quick diagnostic aid to decide if change is possible. Organisational Development can bring approaches to the organization that will enable these three components to surface, so we can begin the process of change. Action Research is a process which serves as a model for most Organisational Development interventions. French, W., & Bell, C., Jr (1990) describe Action Research as a "process of systematically collecting research data about an ongoing system relative to some objective, goal, or need of that system; feeding these data back into the system; taking actions by altering selected variables within the system based both on the data and on hypotheses; and evaluating the results of actions by collecting more data." The steps in Action Research (see page 95 seven-phase consulting model 6, 7).

2.77. Definition of Terms

For a clearer understanding of the views and analysis expressed in this research work, some words, group of words, concepts and terms frequently used interdependently have been define in this section. Such words, group of words, concepts and terms are:

S/no.	Term	Definitions
1.	Associated with Incorporated Trustee	An association of persons, which appoints one or more trustee and pursue registration under Private Company(PC) of the Companies and Allied Matter Act, is called an association with Incorporated trustee.
2.	Company Limited by Guarantee	A company Limited by Guarantee is formed for the promotion of commerce, art, science, religion, sports, culture, education, research, charity, or other similar objectives.
3.	CITA	Company Income Tax Act
4.	VAT	Value Added Tax
5.	SIBR	State Inland Board of Revenue
6.	CAMA	Company and Allied Matter Act
7.	CAC	Corporate Affairs Commission
8.	NGO	Non- Governmental Organisation
9.	NPC	National Population Comission
10.	GDP	Gross Domestic Product
11.	NEPC	Nigeria Export Promotion Council

References

Aukerman, John H.,(1991). Competencies Needed for Effective Ministry by Beginning Pastors in Church of God Congregations in the United States, Unpublished Doctoral Dissertation, Ball State University.

Abdulahi Taiwo Co. Solicitors (1993): Establishing a Business in Nigeria. 4th Edition (Lagos
Academy Press Plc).

Adegbite E. O. (1995), Effective Growth and Survival of Small and Medium ScaleEnterprisesin the 1990s and Beyond. The Role of Policy in Ade T. Ojo (eds) Management of SMEs inNigeria (Lagos Punmark Nig. Ltd)

Anyanwu C. M. (2001): Financing and Promoting Small Scale Industries, Concepts, Issues and
Prospects. Bullion Publication of CBN Vol. 25 No. 3. pp 12 – 15.

Ayozie D. O., Asolo A. A. (1999):Small Scale Business for Nigerian Students (Danayo Inc.
Coy) Ogun State Nigeria.

Ayozie D. O. (1999), Small Scale Business and NationalDevelopment. Conference paper delivered at the CAB, Kaduna Polytechnic, Management Conference.

Ajayi G. O. (2000) Entrepreneurship Development in Nigeria.

Brown, A. C. (1990).Eastern Europe : A Dilemma for the Strategic Planner. Quarterly Review
of Marketing, Autumn.

Balfour, D. L., & Marini, F. (1991). Child and adult, X and Y: Reflections on the process of
public administration education. Public Administration Review, 51 (6), 478-485.

Blockhard,R, &Harris, R. T. (1987). Organizational transitions: Managing complex change.

Block, P.(1981). Flawless consulting: A guide to getting Your expertise used.

Burke,W.W.(1982). Organizational Development: Principles and practices.

Burke, W. W. (1994). Organization development: A process of learning and changing.

Burke, W. W. &Litwin, G. H.(1992). A casual model of organizational performance and change. Journal of management, 18, 523-545.

Bennis, Warren, (1985). Leaders: The Strategies for Taking Charge. Harper and Row, New York,

Brown, J. Truman, Jr.(1984).Church Planning a Year at a Time, (Convention Press, Nashville,).

Burns, Cynthia F. and Carle M. Hunt. (1995). Journal of Ministry, Marketing & Management:

Planning and Ministry Effectiveness in the Church. 1(2) 97-114.

Cheatham, Leo and Carole Cheatham (1995). Journal of Ministry, Marketing & Management:

Budgeting - Part II: Resource Allocation, Planning, and Expenditure Control. 1(2) 73-87.

Clinton, Roy J., Stan Williams, and Robert E. Stevens. (1995). Journal of Ministry Marketing &

Management: Constituent Surveys as an Input in the Strategic Planning Process for Churches and Ministries: Part I. 1(2) 43-55.

Considine, John J. (1996). Journal of Ministry Marketing & Management: Attracting Baby Boomers Back to the Church. 2(1) 33-45.

Church, A. H. (2000). The future of OD: Relevant or not? Presentation to the best practices in leading change conference.

Church, A. H. (2000). Managing change from the inside out. Performance in practice, pp.13-14.

Church, A. H, Burke, W.W. (1995). Practiceitioner attitudes about the field of organization development.

Church, A. H, Hurley, R. F., & Burke, W.W.(1992). Evolution or revolution in the values of organization Development! Commentary on the state of the field. Journal of organizational change management, 5 (4), 6-23.

Church, A. H.& Van Eynde, D. F.(1994). Values, motives, and interventions of organization development practitioners. Group and organization management, 19,5-50.

Cummings T. G., & Worley C. (1993). Organization Development and Change.

Cunningham, J. B. & Eberle, T. (1990). "A Guide to Job Enrichment and Redesign," Personnel.

Davis, K. (1993). Organization Behavior: Human Behavior at Work. New York: McGraw-Hill.

David, F. R. (2003).Concepts of Strategic Management, 9th Edition (Prentice-Hall, Upper Saddle River, NJ,

Drucker P. F. (1985): Innovation and Entrepreneurship. Practice and Principles (London

Heinemman)

Easien O. E. (2001): The role of Development Finance Institutions (DFIs) in the financing ofSmall Scale Industries (SSIs) Bullion Publication of Central Bank of Nigeria Vol. 25 No. 3 pp 36.

Entrepreneurship Development Programme for Youth Corp members (EDP,1990) : NYSC

Publication, Lagos Nigeria.

Fagenson, E. A., Burke, W. W.(1990). The activities of organization development practitioners at the turn of the decade of the 1990s: A Study of their prediction. Group and organization studies, 15, 366-380.

Franklin, J. E., & Freeland, D. K. (1989). Collaborating with McGregor and ASTD. Paper presented at the Annual Meeting of the American Association for Adult and Continuing Education, Atlantic City, NJ.

Federal Republic of Nigeria's company and allied matters Act (CAMA,1990)

French,W. L; Bell, C. H. Jr. (1978). Organization Development: Behavioral science interventions for organization improvement.

Friedlander.(1976). OD reaches adolescence: An exploration of its underlying values. Journal of Applied Behavioral science, 12, 7-21.

Gellerman, W., Frankel,M.S & Ladenson,R. F.(1990). Values and ethics in organization and human systems development: Responding to dilemmas in professional life.

Golembiewski, R.T.(1989). Organization development: Ideas and issues.

Golembiewski, R. T, & Sun, B. C.(1990). Positive findings bias in QWL studies: Rigor and outcomes in a large sample. Journal of management,16,665-674.

Greirier, L.(1980), OD values and the "Bottom Line.

Gangel, Kenneth O.(1989).Feeding and Leading, (SP Publications, Wheaton,).

George, Carl F. (1992).Repare Your Church for the Future, (Fleming H. Revell, Grand Rapids,).

Hackman, J. R. & Oldham, G. R. (1975). "Development of the Job Diagnostic Survey." Journal of Applied Psychology, 60, pp. 159-70.

Johnson, Benton, Dean R. Hoge, and Donald A. Luidens. (1993). First Things: Mainline Churches: The Real Reason for Decline. 31(March) 13-18.

Kegin, James L.(1991). Developing Pastoral Leadership and Management Skills, Unpublished Doctoral Dissertation, Oral Roberts University,

Knoster, T., Villa, R. & Thousand, J. (2000). A framework for thinking about systems change.

Koch, C. (2006). The New Science of Change. CIO Magazine, Sep 15, 2006 (pp 54-56).

Knowles, M. (1978). The adult learner: A neglected species (2nd ed.). Houston, TX: Gulf Publishing.

Mcmahan, G.C. & Church, A. H.(1996). The practice of organization and human resources development in America's fastest growing firms. Leadership and organization development Journal, 19(2), 17-33.

McHennry, J., & Mckenna, D.(1998).Organization Development in high performing companies: An in depth work at the role of OD in microsoft. Organization Development Journal,16, (3), 51-64.

Obitayo K. M. (2001): Creating and Enabling Environment for Small Scale Industries. Bullion Publication of CBN. Vol. 25 No. 3. pp. 116 – 27

Revans, R. W. (1982).The Origin and Growth of Action Learning. Hunt, England: Chatwell-Bratt, Beckley.

Rothwell, W., Sullivan, R., & McLean, G.(1995)."Models for Change and Steps in Action Research", in Practicing OD: A Guide for Consultants, Pfeiffer, San Diego, , pp. 51-69.

Rouda, R. & Kusy, M., Jr. (1995)."Needs assessment - the first step", Tappi Journal 78_(6): 255.

Schein, E. (1968). "Organizational Socialization and the Profession of Management," Industrial Management Review, 1968 vol. 9 pp. 1-15 in Newstrom.

Siegal, W.& Waclawski, J.(1996). Will the real OD practitioners please stand up? A call for change in the field. Organization Development Journal, 14(2), 5-14.

Sievers, B. (1994). Work, death, and life itself. New York: de Gruyter.

Shokan O. (2000). Small Scale Business in Nigeria. (Shone Publishers, Lagos Nigeria)

Tijani-Alawe B. A. (1999). Corporate Governance of Commonwealth Organisation towardsNational Development. A case study of Nigeria Cascon Journal of Management. Vol. 18 Nos. 1& 2 pp. 78- 89

Timmreck, C. W. & A.H. Church (Eds).The handbook of multisource feedback: The comprehensive resources for designing and implementing msf process(pp.301-317).

Tijani-Alawe (2004): Entrepreneurship Processes and Small Business Management. Industrial Science Centre, Owoyemi House, Abeokuta Raod Sango Otta, Ogun State Nigeria.

Tijani-Alawe (2002). Contemporary Lessons in African Philosophy of Business.AbribasExperience in Maternally Moderated Aggressive Fatalism International. Journal of Social andPolicy Issues. Vol. 1 No. 1 pp 59 – 66.Corpus Christi, Texas.

Walters P. G. (1990). Characteristics of successful organization development: A review of literature.

Waclawski, J, &Church, A. H. (1998). The vendor mind set: The devolution from organizational consultant to street peddler. Consulting psychology Journals practice and research,5(2), 87-100.

Waclawski, J,& Burke, W. W.(2000). Multisource fee-back for organization development and change.

Weisbord, M. R. (1987). Productive workplaces. San Francisco: Jossey-Bass.

CHAPTER THREE

3.0.Research Design and Methodology

3.1.Introduction

For the purpose of this research work, this chapter is concerned with the method of collecting information which are of paramount importance and successful completion of this thesis. The researcher made use of textbooks of various authors and papers presented at various seminars on nonprofit sector and organizational development. Holiness Power Bible Ministries is headquartered in Lagos with 40 to 50 branches all over the south-East geopolitical zone in Nigeria. Several churches were also visited which are relevant to the study in other to get facts for the purpose of the subject matter.

3.2.Research Design(Plan of Study)

This formed the framework and plan of this study. The research was carried out in Lagos state where Holiness power Bible Ministries is headquartered. The survey method therefore gave the researcher the opportunity of using many samples to represent the diverse element of the population study. The act of generalization from the sample to the whole population was also enhanced for the researcher. The researcher design was based on the hypothesis which are the statements that could be seen as problems to be examined and tested statistically. They are tentative generalizations that are to be tested on the basis of compatibility of their implications with the empirical evidence and with previous knowledge. They serve as an interpretation of practical situations. This researcher's understanding of the subject matter and the analysis of the literature review are based on the following Null and Alternative questions:

Though in the questionnaire administered fifteen questions (15) were asked but eventually summarized into fourteen (14) in this design which are going to be tested in the later chapter.

3.3. Sampling Procedure/Design

The fact that the research work will tentatively concentrate on Holiness Power Bible Ministries headquartered in Lagos and other branches within and without Lagos state made the sampling very relevant. The targeted respondents in which the questionnaire is to be administered are the pastors, leaders, various committee members of the church both in Holiness power Bible Ministries and other churches, members who have been in the church for about three (3) to five (5) years. It is assumed here that any person who has been in a church within this period is a member of a church irrespective of their denominations or church they attend. In the light of this, it would be easy to reach and collect valid and reliable data, for example, there are over forty (40) branches of Holiness Power Bible Ministries in the South-Eastern Zone of the country Nigeria and over 1.2million of churches in Nigeria.

S/NO.	NULL(Ho)	ALTERNATIVE(Hi)
1.	The church has a mission statement	The church does not have a mission statement.
2.	The church mission statement has made a tremendous difference	The church mission statement has not make any difference.
3.	The church is structured to fulfill the mission of the church	The church is not structured to fulfill the mission of the church.
4.	The church is engaged in long-range planning	The church does not engaged in long-range planning
5.	The church has a written strategic plans	The church does not have any written strategic plans.
6.	The church has a long-range planning committee	The church does not have a long-range planning committee
7.	The committee has been in a existence for a long time	The committee has not been in a existence for a long time.
8.	There is weekly activity days for the church	There is no weekly activity days for the church
9.	There is attendance recorded at the church weekly combine service in the month of July, 2010	There is no average attendance at the weekly combine service in the month of July,2010
10.	The church is growing	The church is not growing
11.	There is average attendance at the last Sunday combine service in the month of July,2010	There is no average attendance at the last Sunday combine service in the month of July,2010

The researcher is compelled to select from among churches in Nigeria, "Holiness Power Bible Ministries" to administer considering the time and other constraints. The church was used as a measure of other churches of similar nature in Nigeria since they have the same aims and objectives of achieving corporate goals(Transparency, probity and Accountability).The implementation and operations may differ to the peculiar nature of the church, but not relevant to this study. The table below shows the percentage distribution of the questionnaire sent out and those returned.

3.4. Distribution of Questionnaire

S/NO.	Survey	No. of copies Sent out	% of copies Sent out	No. of copies Returned	% of copies Returned
1.	Holiness Power Bible Ministries- Headquarter, Lagos	22	31%	18	26%
2.	Ancient Landmark Bible Church-Lagos	18	26%	17	24%
3.	Deeper Life Bible Church(Local/District)	11	16%	9	13%
4.	The Redeemed Church of God(Satellite Churches)	19	27%	19	27%
	Total	70	100%	63	90%

From the above table, it is clearly obvious that only sixty three (63) out of seventy (70) questionnaires representing 90% of the questionnaires distributed were returned. In all, s fifteen(15) questions were asked and answers were fully and adequately given to them. The answers given by the respondent were only different in the use of words but the concept are the same.

3.5. Questionnaire Design

In consideration of the fact that multiple sets of people are involved, the questionnaire was design to be so easy and simple in order to avoid low response in filling all the necessary answers so that inference to be generalized will be so adequate to represent result that is expected to achieve the desired church growth, improved relationship among members of the church and leaders and also the financial condition of the church.

3.6. Data Collection Procedure

Data collection from the respondents were analysed by the use of "YES or NO" which the allocated figures to each of the possible answer are as stated below:

YES	NO
3	2

The mean score is arrived at by multiplying the number of responses in each category by the figures allocated them and dividing the total by the number of responses. This will further be discussed in the next chapter where the analysis will be clearly shown.

The researcher made use of the following sources of data collection for the purpose of achieving the relevant information considered necessary for this thesis.

- Primary data
- Secondary data

(A).Primary Data

This comprises the questionnaire and oral interview with the respondents.

- ***Questionnaires:*** These are the series of pre-printed questions in the questionaire which are structured in form of close and open questions with alternative answers of YES or NO where necessary for the respondents to tick where he/she considered that the system operating are in use. It guides and saves the respondent's time and thinking of which answers are to give to each question in terms of writing.
- ***Personal Interviews and Discussions:*** This was carried out as a supplementary to the questionnaire. The aim is to have direct discussion with different categories of pastors,leaders and members from different churches of of similar nature on areas that technical terms are used by explaining what it means for them to tick the appropriate box and also to save respondent's time and rate of non-responses to those questions asked in the questionnaire. Furthermore, some of the pastors and members prefer the oral interview for the investigator to get more facts which are not in the questions but relevant to the study. This process also allow the writer to question more on the area where no answers were given in the questionnaire in order to know more facts which the respondent intend to conceal. This played a vital and very important role in the conduct of this research. It provided a lot of information which would be necessary for this research.

(B) Secondary Data

These are also those data that have been used for some purposes other than that for which they were originally collected. For the purpose of this research the researcher make use of paper presented on Non-profit organization and Organisational development and textbooks on related topics in the research work.

3.7.0. Statistical Tools of Analysis Employed

For the purpose of this research, based on the fact that proposed analysis would be on bivariate associative data, the research was conducted by questionnaire and personal interview with the respondent. A point by point is considered in the analysis of the responses of the questionnaire and Interview which was made by the use of description method. The researcher tries as much as possible to clearly state the views gathered and generalization of opinions derived was made where necessary. Many analytical methods can be used but among the commonly used ones is Chi-Square test which is most appropriate for this study.

3.7.1. The raison dêtre for using this analytical method are:

a). The questions are categorized in a way under which the respondents to whom the data collection instruments were administered would give "YES" or " NO" responses.

b). The data to be collected are non-metric. The Null hypothesis (Ho) is hereby restated. This means that in Ho: there is significant improvement which makes greater efficiency and effectiveness in the solving organizational development problem in the non-profit sector.

The following formula is used in computing the Chi-Square (X^2) test value for the data.

$X^2 = \Sigma \underline{(0\text{-}E)}^2$

2

Where X^2 = Chi-Square

0 = Observed Frequency
E = Expected Frequency
Σ = Summation 2

Expected frequency (E) is derived by taking the probability of getting each cell in the whole distribution while, Observed frequency (0) is the actual response of the total respondents.

3.8. Constraints

In most cases or occasions, the General- Overseer's (Church founders) were not available and when they were on seat, they tend to be much busy as to even have time to answer some questions. In such cases some opted to interview to answering the questionnaires which the researcher has to do a lot of writings. More so, many of the respondent lost the questionnaire given to them and some did not return theirs and some did not fill the questionnaires adequately.

Secondly, due to financial constraints a wider coverage in the area of the study was prevented.

References

Afonja.B (1982).Introductory Statistics on a Leaner's Motivate Approach: Evan Brothers (Nigeria Publishers) Limited, Jericho Road Ibadan.

Fatunla G.T(1996). Statistical Method for Business and Technology: Truevine Nig Ltd (Publisher),Akure.

Leonard J. Kazmier,(1976).Schaum's Outline Series Theory and Problems of Business Statistic: Mcgraw-Hill Book Company(Publisher) p.195-203.

Nnamdi,Asika,(1991).Research Methodology in the Behavioural Sciences: Longman Nigeria

Plc(Publisher).

Walpole R.E,(1982). Introduction to Statistic: Third Edition-Macmillan Publishing Co. Inc.886 Third Avenue, New York.

CHAPTER FOUR

4.0. Data Analysis and Research Findings

4.1. Collection of data

The collection of data for this research work was achieved by the use of questionnaires and oral interviews. The questionnaire contains part 1, which consist of personal data such as: Age, Status/Position held in the Church and period he/she joined the church (experience) while the oral interview was centered on the various pastors and leaders from other churches and denominations. Attempt would be made to classify respondents of the same sections of work in the church to ascertain if, for example all respondents from the church give similar responses to the same sets of questions. This chapter would also answer the research questions posed under the section tilled research questions. In addition, decision would be taken on accepting or rejecting the Null hypothesis.

4.2. Analysis of data

The table 4.1 below represents the data analysis Classification of Personal data

Variables	Answers	Number of Responses	Percentage of Responses %
Age	21-25	12	19%
	26-30	7	11%
	31-35	8	12%
	36-40	19	30%
	40 and above	17	26%
	Total	63	26%
Status/Position	Vetting committee-members	6	9%
	Marriage committee-Members	7	11%
	House Leaders	35	55%
	pastors	10	15%
	Total	63	90
Years of church membership	Below 10 years	15	23%
	Between 10-20 years	29	46%
	Between 20-30 years	11	17%
	Between 30 and above	3	4%
	Total	63	90%
Sex	Male	39	61%
	Female	24	38%
	Total	63	99%

Source: Primary data

The table above fully stated the purpose of differences in perception, the following examples will be of help.

Age: 12(19%) out of 63 persons are between the ages of 21-25 years; 7 (11%) are between 26-30 years; 8(12%) are between 31-35 years; 19 (30%) are between 36-40 years; while 17 (26%) only are 40 and above.

The average age of the people that represent the sample size of the research on organizational development in Holiness Power Bible Ministries is calculated as follows:

Table 4.2 Means age of pastors and members

Age	Mid-Point(X)	Frequency(F)	FX
21-25	23	12	276
26-30	28	7	196
31-35	33	8	264
36-40	38	19	722
40 and above	43	17	731
	Total	63	2189

Mean = x = $\underline{\sum fx}$
$\sum f$
= $\underline{2189}$
63

= 34.7 or 35 years approximately.

Also the mean (average) years of church membership sample in Holiness power Bible Ministries is calculated thus:

$$\text{Mean} = X = \frac{\sum fx}{\sum f} = \frac{885}{63} = 14 \text{ years}$$

4.3. Discussions

For the purpose of this study, the Chi-Square (X^2) method is used to test the validity of the hypothesis. The Chi-square is a measure of the discrepancy existing between observed and expected frequencies. The Null hypothesis is been tested. The decision rule is to accept the Null hypothesis if the X^2 calculated is less than the table Chi-Square and reject the Null hypothesis if the X^2 calculated is greater than the table Chi-Square.

The formula for calculating Chi-Square is:

$$X^2 = \frac{\sum\{O-E\}^2}{E}$$

Where X^2 = Chi-Square
O = Observed frequency
E = Expected frequency
Σ = "Summation"²

Expected frequency (E) of a cell is derived as:

$$\frac{\text{(ROW Total) (Column Total)}}{\text{Grand Total}}$$

4.4. Degree of freedom (df)

Degree of freedom is defined as the number "R" of independent observation in the sample size multiply by the " K" of the population parameters estimated from sample observations.

Thus df = (R-I)(K-I)
Where R= Row

K= Column

The df for the purpose of testing the hypothesis in this study, therefore is:

(R-I) (K-)

(2-1) (3-1

(1) (2)

= 1ˣ2 = 2

Using 0.05 level of significance,X^2 at 0.95 where df is 2= 5.99147

Hypothesis 1

Null (Ho). The church has a mission statement.

Alternative (Hi). The church does not have a mission statement.

Question 5 on the questionnaire is used to test this hypothesis calculated X^2 = 2.2257 at a0.0s level, the difference is significant if X^2 with 2 degree of freedom is 5.99. Hence, the computed value of X^2 which is 2.2257 is than the critical value and falls within the acceptance region. Thus, the Null hypothesis (Ho) is valid. To further prove its validity 48 out of 63 respondents say "YES". While 15 say "NO" and 3 persons neither say YES or NO.

Hypothesis 2

NULL(Ho). The church mission statement has made a tremendous difference

Alternative(Hi). The church mission statement has not make any difference.

Question 6 on the questionnaire is used to test this hypothesis. Calculated X^2 = 5.251at a 0.05 level, the difference is significant if X^2 with 2 degree of freedom is 5.99. Hence, the calculated value X^2 =5.251 is lesser than the critical value and falls within the acceptable region. Thus, the Null hypothesis(Ho) is valid. To further prove its validity 51 out of 63 respondents say YES, while only 12 says NO.

Hypothesis 3

NULL(Ho). The church is structured to fulfill the mission of the church

Alternative (Hi). The church is not structured to fulfill the mission of the church.

Question 7 on the questionnaire is relevant for the testing of this hypothesis. Calculated $X^2 = 3.4937$ at 5% level, the difference is significant if X^2 with degree of freedom is above 5.99. The Calculated value of X^2 which is smaller than the critical value and falls within the acceptable region. Thus the Null hypothesis(Ho) is valid. To validate the result, it is discovered that a total of 53 persons out of 63 respondents agree, while 10 persons say No.

Hypothesis 4

NULL (Ho). The church is engaged in long-range planning

Alternative (Hi). The church does not engaged in long-range planning

Question 8 0n the questionnaire is used to test the hypothesis. Calculated $X^2 = 3.1916$ at a 0.05 level is calculated to be 13.0445, the difference is significant if X^2 with 2 degree of freedom is more than 5.99. The calculated value of X^2 which is 13.0445 is greater than the critical value and hence, should be rejected. Therefore, the Null hypothesis (Ho) is rejected. Thus, Null hypothesis (Ho) is invalid. To validate the results, it is discovered that a total of 40 respondents confirmed No, while only 23 say Yes.

Hypothesis 5

NULL (Ho). The church has written strategic plans

Alternative (Hi). The church does not have any written strategic plans.

Question 9 on the questionnaire is used o test this hypothesis. Calculated X^2 at a 0.05 level is calculated to be 15.98519; the difference is significant if X^2 with 2 degree of freedom is more than 5.99. The calculated value of X^2 which is 15.98519 is greater than the critical value and hence, should be rejected. Thus, Null hypothesis (Ho) is invalid. Furthermore, a total of 43 respondents confirmed No, while 20 persons say Yes..

Hypothesis 6

NULL (Ho). The church has a long-range planning committee

Alternative (Hi). The church does not have a long-range planning committee

Question 10 on the questionnaire is used in testing the validity of this hypothesis. The calculated X^2 = 27.77643 at a 0.05 level, the difference is significant if X^2 with 2 degree of freedom is above 5.99. The calculated value of X^2 which is 27.77643 is greater than the critical value and hence, should be rejected. Thus, the Null hypothesis (Ho) is invalid. To further prove of its validity, a total of 49 persons out of 63 respondents say No, while 14 say Yes.

Hypothesis 7

NULL (Ho). The committee has been in a existence for a long time

Alternative (Hi). The committee has not been in a existence for a long time.

Question 12 on the questionnaire is used to test this hypothesis. The calculated X^3 =29.26713 at a , 0.05 level, the difference is significant if X^2 with 2 degree of freedom is 5.99. Hence, the computed value of X^2 which is 29.26713 is greater than the critical value, hence should be rejected. Therefore, the Null hypothesis (Ho) is rejected and invalid. To prove further the authenticity of the result, a total of 50 respondents out of 63 confirmed No. while only 13 say Yes.

Hypothesis 8

NULL(Ho). There is weekly activity days for the church

Alternative(Hi). There is no weekly activity days for the church

Question 13 on the questionnaire is used to test this hypothesis. The Calculated X^2 =3.4937 at 0.05 level, the difference is significant if the X^2 with 2 degree of freedom is above 5.99. The calculated value of X^2 which is 3.4937 is smaller than the critical value and falls within the acceptable region. Therefore, the Null Hypothesis (Ho) is accepted as valid. To prove the validity of the result further, a total of 53 persons out of 63 respondents says Yes. While 10 says No.

Hypothesis 10

NULL (Ho). The church is growing

Alternative (Hi). The church is not growing

Question 14,15 and 16 on the questionnaire were used in testing the validity of this Hypothesis. The calculated X^2 at a 0.05 level is calculated to be 29.26713; the difference is significant if X^2 with 2 degree of freedom is 5.99. The calculated value of X^2 which is 29.26713 is greater than the critical value and therefore should be rejected; the Null hypothesis (Ho) is invalid. To prove the authenticity of the result a total of 50 out of 63 respondents confirmed No. while only 13 says Yes.

Hypothesis 12

NULL(Ho). There is overall change in the church membership in the last two years

Alternative (Hi). There is no change in the church membership in the last two years

Question 17,18 and 19 on the questionnaire is used to test this hypothesis. The calculated X^2 at 5% level is calculated to be 13.04446 , the difference is significant if X^2 with 2 degree of freedom is more than 5.99.The calculated value of X^2 which is 13.04446 is greater than the critical value and should be rejected. The Null hypothesis (Ho) is rejected and therefore invalid. To prove further the result a total of 40 respondents says NO while 23 says YES.

Hypothesis 13

NULL (Ho). There is overall change in the church's financial condition in the last two years

Alternative (Hi). There is no improvement in the church financial condition in the last two years

Question 19, 20 and 21 were used in testing this hypothesis. Calculated X^2 at a 0.05 level is calculated to be 27.77643; the difference is significant if X^2 with 2 degree of freedom is more than 5.99. The calculated value of X^2 which is 27.77643 is greater than the critical value and hence, should be rejected. Thus, Null hypothesis (Ho) is invalid. Furthermore, a total of 49 respondents confirmed No, while 14 persons neither say Yes or No.

Hypothesis 14

NULL(Ho). Other persons are involved in deciding upon overall church direction and expenditures except the General Overseer himself.

Alternative(Hi). The pastors and church leaders are not involved in deciding upon overall church direction and expenditures.

Question 23 on the questionnaire is used to this hypothesis. The calculated X^2 at 5% level is calculated to be 13.04446, the difference is significant if X^2 with 2 degree of freedom is more than 5.99.The calculated value of X^2 which is 13.04446 is greater than the critical value and should be rejected. The Null hypothesis (Ho) is rejected and therefore invalid. To prove further the result a total of 40 respondents says No while 23 says YES.

4.5.Table 4.3 Summary of Statement By Respondents
Total Score and Mean X Score(N=63)

<Insert image jpg 4.5Here>

CHAPTER FIVE

5.0. Summary, Recommendations and Conclusion

5.1. Introduction

This chapter is bringing into focus the data earlier analysed in chapter four. It is mostly concerned with the summary of my research work which is to examine organizational development problems in the nonprofit sector with particular reference to "Holiness Power Bible Church" headquartered in Lagos, Nigeria with a view of solving the problems by a way of proffering suitable solutions capable of improving the organization.

5.2.0. Summary of the Study

The research work concerned itself with "Solving organizational development problems in the non-profit sector" with particular reference to "Holiness Power Bible Ministries "in Lagos. It consists the areas covered on organizational development and nonprofit sector which contain thus, after a brief introduction, the historical background of Holiness Power Bible Ministries was highlighted. The features of statement of the problems (Rationale for choice of the subject matter), the purpose of the study, Research questions, significance of the study and the scope of and limitations of this study were stated. Data collection and plan of study as well as references cited were stated. Some literature relevant to the study was later enunciated. Personal interview was later conducted by the researcher to elicit information from selected General Overseer(New church founders) and pastors of branch and satellite churches on the study and analysis of information received from the questionnaire was also made use of. The researcher also made use of tables to clearly illustrate some salient point to ease the understanding of the readers.

5.2.1.Research Findings

The finding from both responses received from questionnaire and interview with the pastors and members of Holiness Power Bible Ministries and pastors and members of other denominations revealed that the following were observed:

- It was discovered from my analysis that both pastors in the headquarters and branch churches of Holiness Power Bible Ministries and in other denominations say NO to many of the questions asked indicating total and absolute dissatisfaction of the present situation in the church.
- It was discovered through one on one interview that members do complained about some Utterances of the General Overseer from the

pulpit which they describe as been scaring and as a result church keep decreasing.

- Lack of sound internal control or effective management in the area of budget implementation was found to be the major reasons why most newly nonprofit organization are having serious financial problems as the founders syndrome plays overwhelming role.
- When interviewing the full-time workforce of the church it was revealed to me that they are being owed their salary for some months now and that they are being in arrears instead of monthly bases as obtainable in most bigger nonprofit organizations.
- It was discovered that Organisational Development is best served in the larger churches than in the newly formed churches as in the case of "Holiness Power Bible Ministries."
- It was discovered as well that different churches operates in different ways according to the leadership style of the church founder. Some founders are autocratic in approach; while some are people oriented which gives them leverage over the autocratic leaders.
- The General Overseer of Holiness Power Bible Ministries is a very aggressive and autocratic preacher which culminated to his actions being misinterpreted as either claiming to have sole authority of the word of God.
- It was also discovered that primary six certificate holders and s.75 are more in numbers than degree holders and this otherwise affected the organization of the church as capable hands are not on ground to make meaning contributions

towards the development of the church(Holiness Power Bible Church in particular) unlike the bigger churches.

- Holiness Power Bible Ministries is widely known as "Operation Tikpo" which is been translated in English as "Operation destroy the works of the devil."
- Some pastors in the (HPBM) revealed that there is always pastoral meetings almost every Sunday but the outcome of the meetings are never implement in the church indicating that the GO dominates in every issues that has to with the church and as a result pastors are just following sheepishly.
- HBPM has a smaller cells of about 5 to 10 members(Known as Power house fellowship) in all the regions in Lagos state which are meant to grow and multiply into various groups thereby enhancing church growth which are not functioning if not dead.

5.2.3. Other findings include;

- Holiness Power Bible Ministries is heavily dependent of Tithes and Offerings and little contributions from members of the church who came to the church for help as well.
- The General Overseer has turned down many gift and donations with reason that he must hear from God before accepting those gift and this in turn has affected the financial state of the church as people are skeptical of giving to the church (HPBM).

- Church programmes and other activities like outdoor crusades are heavily underfunded as no other source of income to the church except for tithe and offering.
- Many churchgoers feel that church is out of touch with them and has not responded to their needs. Organisational development can be used to stem this negative trend.
- lack of organizational development can be attributed as the cause for many churches' failures in achieving their ministerial and organizational goals. To compound this problem, many churches today are facing declining membership and attendance levels as numerous activities divert individuals away from church.
- The findings indicate that church that incorporate organizational development are more likely to achieve higher growth rates in membership. Organisational development allows a church to address the needs of its members and the community.
- That Organisational development will help churches experience higher rates of growth in finances than those who do not embrace it.
- That financial condition improved at the same rate as membership increases too.
- Organisational development may contribute to churches increasing in size.

5.3. Recommendations

Going through the theme of the research work and as presented in the analysis and evaluation, the proffered recommendations could be drawn which are as follow:

- Poor attitude of pastors and leaders have been notice to be the major factor inhibiting effective implementation of budgetary control, therefore a good working relationship must be develop among top church leaders and their subordinates to pave way to successful budgetary implementation.
- Church leaders should be provided with the training and skills needed to incorporate Organisational development in their ministries.
- Holiness Power should identify the needs of the community; set goals for meeting those needs, and formulate a plan for achieving those goals.
- Membership will grow when the community feels that the church is meeting and addressing their needs.(Acts.6:1)
- The satellite pastors and their state counterparts should be adequately motivated monetarily and otherwise in other to discourage any form of stealing from the church purse. This is important because the aspiration of those implementing plans is not usually not the same as corporate objective of the church.
- Lastly, Organisational development, help to meet the growing aspirations of the members and assist in finding solutions to the increasing

challenges facing nonprofit organizations, especially, the churches.

5.4. Conclusion

From the foregoing, the following conclusions can be drawn concerning the sample Churches:

- Most smaller churches in Nigeria do not engage in organizational development.
- Organisational development has a positive effect on church membership growth rates and financial Condition.
- Larger churches are more likely to engage in Organisational development,but there is no reason that these same activities cannot be implemented in smaller churches with similar Success.

The pastor (General Overseer or Founder) of a church is the primary person relied upon to provide direction and leadership in the planning and decision making process within the church. As a church faces declining numbers in both members and finances, methods must be employed to address these issues. Organization development is an ongoing, systematic process to implement effective change in an organization. Through organizational development, a church can map an approach for meeting the goals and objectives they have established. Churches are relied upon to provide training, counseling, leadership and direction for their congregations and communities. They must serve their members in a constantly changing world. To effectively address these many responsibilities, it is essential that a church engage in organizational development.

Organisational development can provide direction for meeting these challenges and can help eliminate the frustration that results from a lack of direction.

References

Afonja.B (1982).Introductory Statistics on a Leaner's Motivate Approach: Evan Brothers (Nigeria Publishers) Limited, Jericho Road Ibadan

Aukerman, John H.,(1991). Competencies Needed for Effective Ministry by Beginning Pastors in Church of God Congregations in the United States, Unpublished Doctoral Dissertation, Ball State University.

Abdulahi Taiwo Co. Solicitors (1993): Establishing a Business in Nigeria. 4th Edition (Lagos

Academy Press Plc).

Adegbite E. O. (1995), Effective Growth and Survival of Small and Medium ScaleEnterprisesin the 1990s and Beyond. The Role of Policy in Ade T. Ojo (eds) Management of SMEs inNigeria (Lagos Punmark Nig. Ltd)

Anyanwu C. M. (2001): Financing and Promoting Small Scale Industries, Concepts, Issues and

Prospects. Bullion Publication of CBN Vol. 25 No. 3. pp 12 – 15.

Ayozie D. O., Asolo A. A. (1999):Small Scale Business for Nigerian Students (Danayo Inc.

Coy) Ogun State Nigeria.

Ayozie D. O. (1999), Small Scale Business and NationalDevelopment. Conference paper delivered at the CAB, Kaduna Polytechnic, Management Conference.

Ajayi G. O. (2000) Entrepreneurship Development in Nigeria.

Brown, A. C. (1990).Eastern Europe : A Dilemma for the Strategic Planner. Quarterly Review of Marketing, Autumn.

Brown, J. Truman, Jr.(1984).Church Planning a Year at a Time.Convention Press, Nashville.

Balfour, D. L., & Marini, F. (1991). Child and adult, X and Y: Reflections on the process of public administration education. Public Administration Review, 51 (6), 478-485.

Blockhard,R, &Harris, R. T. (1987). Organizational transitions: Managing complex change.

Block, P.(1981). Flawless consulting: A guide to getting Your expertise used.

Burke,W.W.(1982). Organizational Development: Principles and practices.

Burke, W. W. (1994). Organization development: A process of learning and changing.

Burke, W. W. &Litwin, G. H.(1992). A casual model of organizational performance and change. Journal of management, 18, 523-545.

Bennis, Warren, (1985). Leaders: The Strategies for Taking Charge. Harper and Row, New York,

Brown, J. Truman, Jr.(1984).Church Planning a Year at a Time, (Convention Press, Nashville,).

Burns, Cynthia F. and Carle M. Hunt. (1995). Journal of Ministry, Marketing & Management: Planning and Ministry Effectiveness in the Church. 1(2) 97-114.

Cheatham, Leo and Carole Cheatham (1995). Journal of Ministry, Marketing & Management: Budgeting - Part II: Resource Allocation, Planning, and Expenditure Control. 1(2) 73-87.

Clinton, Roy J., Stan Williams, and Robert E. Stevens. (1995). Journal of Ministry Marketing &

Management: Constituent Surveys as an Input in the Strategic Planning Process for Churches and Ministries: Part I. 1(2) 43-55.

Considine, John J. (1996). Journal of Ministry Marketing & Management: Attracting Baby Boomers Back to the Church. 2(1) 33-45.

Church, A. H. (2000). The future of OD: Relevant or not? Presentation to the best practices in leading change conference.

Church, A. H. (2000). Managing change from the inside out. Performance in practice, pp.13-14.

Church, A. H, Burke, W.W. (1995). Practiceitioner attitudes about the field of organization development.

Church, A. H, Hurley, R. F., & Burke, W.W.(1992). Evolution or revolution in the values of organization Development! Commentary on the state of the field. Journal of organizational change management, 5 (4), 6-23.

Church, A. H.& Van Eynde, D. F.(1994). Values, motives, and interventions of organization development practitioners. Group and organization management, 19,5-50.

Cummings T. G., & Worley C. (1993). Organization Development and Change.

Cunningham, J. B. & Eberle, T. (1990). "A Guide to Job Enrichment and Redesign," Personnel.

Davis, K. (1993). Organization Behavior: Human Behavior at Work. New York: McGraw-Hill.

David, F. R. (2003).Concepts of Strategic Management, 9th Edition (Prentice-Hall, Upper Saddle River, NJ,

Drucker P. F. (1985): Innovation and Entrepreneurship. Practice and Principles (London Heinemman)

Easien O. E. (2001): The role of Development Finance Institutions (DFIs) in the financing ofSmall Scale Industries

(SSIs) Bullion Publication of Central Bank of Nigeria Vol. 25 No. 3 pp 36.

Entrepreneurship Development Programme for Youth Corp members (EDP,1990) : NYSC

Publication, Lagos Nigeria.

Fagenson, E. A., Burke, W. W.(1990). The activities of organization development practitioners at the turn of the decade of the 1990s: A Study of their prediction. Group and organization studies, 15, 366-380.

Fatunla G.T(1996). Statistical Method for Business and Technology: Truevine Nig Ltd (Publisher),Akure

Franklin, J. E., & Freeland, D. K. (1989). Collaborating with McGregor and ASTD. Paper

presented at the Annual Meeting of the American Association for Adult and Continuing Education, Atlantic City, NJ.

Federal Republic of Nigeria's company and allied matters Act (CAMA,1990) French,W. L; Bell, C. H. Jr. (1978). Organization Development: Behavioral science interventions for organization improvement.

Friedlander.(1976). OD reaches adolescence: An exploration of its underlying values. Journal of Applied Behavioral science, 12, 7-21.

Gellerman, W., Frankel,M.S & Ladenson,R. F.(1990). Values and ethics in organization and human systems development: Responding to dilemmas in professional life.

Golembiewski, R.T.(1989). Organization development: Ideas and issues.

Golembiewski, R. T, & Sun, B. C.(1990). Positive findings bias in QWL studies: Rigor and outcomes in a large sample. Journal of management,16,665-674.

Greirier, L.(1980), OD values and the "Bottom Line.

Gangel, Kenneth O.(1989).Feeding and Leading, (SP Publications, Wheaton,).

George, Carl F. (1992).Repare Your Church for the Future, (Fleming H. Revell, Grand Rapids,).

Hackman, J. R. & Oldham, G. R. (1975). "Development of the Job Diagnostic Survey." Journal of Applied Psychology, 60, pp. 159-70.

Holiness Power Bible Ministries (HPBM,2008).The rule and regulations and administrative guideline.

Johnson, Benton, Dean R. Hoge, and Donald A. Luidens. (1993). First Things: Mainline Churches: The Real Reason for Decline. 31(March) 13-18.

Kegin, James L.(1991). Developing Pastoral Leadership and Management Skills, Unpublished Doctoral Dissertation, Oral Roberts University,

Knoster, T., Villa, R. & Thousand, J. (2000). A framework for thinking about systems change.

Koch, C. (2006). The New Science of Change. CIO Magazine, Sep 15, 2006 (pp 54-56).

.Knowles, M. (1978). The adult learner: A neglected species (2nd ed.). Houston, TX: Gulf

Publishing.

Leonard J. Kazmier,(1976).Schaum's Outline Series Theory and Problems of Business Statistic:

Mcgraw-Hill Book Company(Publisher) p.195-203

Maes, Jeanne D. (1998). Journal of Ministry Marketing & Management: I'll Take Parish Strategic Planning,4(1) 25-31.

Mcmahan, G.C. & Church, A. H.(1996). The practice of organization and human resources development in America's fastest growing firms. Leadership and organization development Journal, 19(2), 17-33.

McHennry, J., & Mckenna, D.(1998).Organization Development in high performing companies: An in depth work at the role of OD in microsoft. Organization Development Journal,16, (3), 51-64.

Nnamdi,Asika,(1991).Research Methodology in the Behavioural Sciences: Longman Nigeria Plc(Publisher).

Obitayo K. M. (2001): Creating and Enabling Environment for Small Scale Industries. Bullion Publication of CBN. Vol. 25 No. 3. pp. 116 – 27

Revans, R. W. (1982).The Origin and Growth of Action Learning. Hunt, England: Chatwell-Bratt, Beckley.

Rothwell, W., Sullivan, R., & McLean, G.(1995)."Models for Change and Steps in Action Research", in Practicing OD: A Guide for Consultants, Pfeiffer, San Diego, , pp. 51-69.

Rouda, R. & Kusy, M., Jr. (1995)."Needs assessment - the first step", Tappi Journal 78_(6): 255.

Schein, E. (1968). "Organizational Socialization and the Profession of Management," Industrial Management Review, 1968 vol. 9 pp. 1-15 in Newstrom.

Siegal, W.& Waclawski, J.(1996). Will the real OD practitioners please stand up? A call for change in the field. Organization Development Journal, 14(2), 5-14.

Sievers, B. (1994). Work, death, and life itself. New York: de Gruyter.

Shokan O. (2000). Small Scale Business in Nigeria. (Shone Publishers, Lagos Nigeria)

Tijani-Alawe B. A. (1999). Corporate Governance of Commonwealth Organisation towardsNational Development. A case study of Nigeria Cascon Journal of Management. Vol. 18 Nos. 1& 2 pp. 78- 89

Timmreck, C. W. & A.H. Church (Eds).The handbook of multisource feedback: The comprehensive resources for designing and implementing msf process(pp.301-317).

Tijani-Alawe (2004): Entrepreneurship Processes and Small Business Management. Industrial

Science Centre, Owoyemi House, Abeokuta Raod Sango Otta, Ogun State Nigeria.

Tijani-Alawe (2002). Contemporary Lessons in African Philosophy of Business.AbribasExperience in Maternally Moderated Aggressive Fatalism International. Journal of Social andPolicy Issues. Vol. 1 No. 1 pp 59 – 66.Corpus Christi, Texas.

Walters P. G. (1990). Characteristics of successful organization development: A review of literature.

Waclawski, J, &Church, A. H. (1998). The vendor mind set: The devolution from organizational consultant to street peddler. Consulting psychology Journals practice and research,5(2), 87-100.

Waclawski, J,& Burke, W. W.(2000). Multisource fee-back for organization development and change.

Weisbord, M. R. (1987). Productive workplaces. San Francisco: Jossey-Bass.

Walpole R.E,(1982). Introduction to Statistic: Third Edition-Macmillan Publishing Co. Inc.886 Third Avenue, New York.

APPENDIX I

ATLANTIC INTERNATIONAL UNIVERSITY
HONOLULU, HAWAII,
U.S.A.

Dear Respondent,

Having completed my doctorate degree academic course work as prescribed by the above named institution, I am currently writing my thesis on the topic "Solving Organizational Development Problems in the Non-Profit Sector" with particular reference to "Holiness Power Bible Ministries' Headquartered in Lagos, Nigeria, as requirement for the award of PH.D degree.

In order to accomplish this task, I am hereby humbly requesting that you kindly assist in completing this questionnaire to enable me gain from your wide knowledge and experience about non-profit organization, particularly church administration and development for the betterment of my self, Holiness Power Bible Church where I fellowship and the general public and other organization of similar nature.

All information supplied is meant for academic exercise and will be kept secret.

Thank you sir.
Yours sincerely,
Osemeka C. Anthony
Researcher

APPENDIX II

QUESTIONNAIRE

1. Which denomination of church do you belong?
a. Holiness Power Bible Church
b. Deeper Life Bible Church
c. Ancient Landmark
d. The Redeemed Christian Church of God

Please tick as appropriate for the questions below:

2. Age: i) 21 – 25
ii) 26– 30
iii) 31 – 35
iv) 36 – 40
v) 40 and above

3. Educational/professional qualification
a. Pry School Certificate
b. WASC or equivalent
c. OND/HND
d. B Sc or equivalent
e. Professional qualification (ACCA, ACA , ACIA, ANAN)

4. How long have you been in the church?
a. Below 10years
b. 10 – 20 years
c. 20 – 30 years
d. 30 – 40 years
e. 40 and above

5. Does your church have a mission statement?

Yes ( )
No ( )

6. Does the mission make any difference/

Yes ( )
No ( )

7. Does the church structure to fulfill the mission of the church?

Yes ( )
No ( )

8. Does your church engage in long-range planning?

Yes ( )
No ( )

9. Does your church have written strategic plans?

Yes ( )
No ( )

10. Does your church have a long-range planning committee?

Yes ( )
No ( )

11. Are pastors and leaders involved in the planning process?

Yes ( )
No ( )

12. How long has the committee been in existence?
a. 2 years
b. 5 years
c. 10 years
d. 15 years
e. 20 and above

13. Does your church meet on weekly bases?
Yes ( )
No ( )

14. What are the weekly activity days of your church?
a. Monday
b. Tuesday
c. Wednesday
d. Thursday
e. Friday

15. What is the average attendance at the weekly activities in the month of July, 2010?
a. below 100
b. 200
c. 300
d. above 300

16. What is the average attendance at the Sunday combine service in the month of July, 2010?
a. below 500
b. 600
c. 700
d. above 700

17. Is there decline in membership in the last two years.

Yes ( )
No ( )

18 . Is your church growing
Yes ( )
No ( )

18. How would you describe the overall change in your church's membership presently?
a. increasing greatly
b. increasing sometimes
c. declining sometimes
d. declining greatly

19. How do you describe the overall change in your church's financial condition in the last two years?
a. improving greatly
b. improving sometime
c. declining sometime
d. declining greatly

20. Is the church tithes and offering good enough to cater for the needs of the church?

Yes ( )
No ( )

21. Does you church received external support in a way of grants and donations to meet up with it's financial?

Yes ( )
No ( )

23.Are the pastor and other Leader involved in deciding upon overall church direction and expenditures?

Yes ( )

No ( )

APPENDIX III

Hypothesis 1

Table 1.1. Observed frequency

Reponse	Vetting Committee Members	Marriage Committee Members	Pastors	House Leaders	Total
Yes	6	5	7	30	48
No	-	2	3	10	15
Total	6	7	10	40	63

Source: Primary Data

Hypothesis 2

Table 2.1.Observed frequency

Reponse	Vetting Committee Members	Marriage Committee Members	Pastors	House Leaders	Total
Yes	6	7	15	23	51
No	-	-	5	7	12
Total	6	7	20	30	63

Source: Primary Data

Table 2.2.Expected frequency

Response	Vetting Committee Members	Marriage Committee Members	Pastors	House Leaders	Total
Yes	4.83	5.66	16.19	24.28	51
No	1.15	1.34	3.81	5.72	12
Total	6	7	20	30	63

Source: Primary Data

Hypothesis 3

Table 3.1.Observed frequency

Reponse	Vetting Committee Members	Marriage Committee Members	Pastors	House Leaders	Total
Yes	6	7	20	20	53
No	-	-	4	6	10
Total	6	7	24	26	63

Source: Primary Data

Table 3.2.Expected frequency

Response	Vetting Committee Members	Marriage Committee Members	Pastors	House Leaders	Total
Yes	5.04	5.88	20.19	21.87	53
No	0.96	1.12	3.81	4.13	10
Total	6	7	24	26	63

Source: Primary Data

Hypothesis 4

Table 4.1.Observed frequency

Reponse	Vetting Committee Members	Marriage Committee Members	Pastors	House Leaders	Total
Yes	6	2	9	6	23
No	2	3	7	28	40
Total	8	5	16	34	63

Source: Primary Data

Table 4.2.Expected frequency

Response	Vetting Committee Members	Marriage Committee Members	Pastors	House Leaders	Total
Yes	2.92	1.82	5.84	12.41	23
No	5.07	3.17	10.15	21.58	40
Total	6	5	16	34	63

Source: Primary Data

Hypothesis 5

Table 5.1.Observed frequency

Reponse	Vetting Committee Members	Marriage Committee Members	Pastors	House Leaders	Total
Yes	6	4	3	7	20
No	-	6	7	30	43
Total	6	10	10	37	63

Source: Primary Data

Table 5.2.Expected frequency

Response	Vetting Committee Members	Marriage Committee Members	Pastors	House Leaders	Total
Yes	1.90	3.17	3.17	11.74	20
No	4.09	6.82	6.82	25.25	43
Total	6	10	10	37	63

Source: Primary Data

Hypothesis 6

Table 6.1.Observed frequency

Reponse	Vetting Committee Members	Marriage Committee Members	Pastors	House Leaders	Total
Yes	6	3	3	2	14
No	-	6	8	35	49
Total	6	9	11	37	63

Source: Primary Data

Table 6.2.Expected frequency

Response	Vetting Committee Members	Marriage Committee Members	Pastors	House Leaders	Total
Yes	1.33	2	2.44	8.22	14
No	4.66	7	8.55	28.77	49
Total	6	9	11	37	63

Source: Primary Data

Hypothesis 7

<Insert image jpg table 7.1-3 appendix111Here> NO FILE

Hypothesis 8

Table 8.1.Observed frequency

Reponse	Vetting Committee Members	Marriage Committee Members	Pastors	House Leaders	Total
Yes	6	7	20	20	53
No	-	-	4	6	10
Total	6	7	24	26	63

Source: Primary Data

Table 8.2.Expected frequency

Response	Vetting Committee Members	Marriage Committee Members	Pastors	House Leaders	Total
Yes	5.04	5.88	20.19	21.87	53
No	0.96	1.12	3.81	4.13	10
Total	6	7	24	26	63

Source: Primary Data

Hypothesis 10

Table 10.1.Observed frequency

Reponse	Vetting Committee Members	Marriage Committee Members	Pastors	House Leaders	Total
Yes	6	3	2	2	13
No	-	6	9	35	50
Total	6	9	11	37	63

Source: Primary Data

Table 10.2.Expected frequency

Response	Vetting Committee Members	Marriage Committee Members	Pastors	House Leaders	Total
Yes	1.23	1.85	2.26	7.63	13
No	4.76	7.14	8.73	29.36	50
Total	6	9	11	37	63

Source: Primary Data

Hypothesis 12

Table 12.1.Observed frequency

Reponse	Vetting Committee Members	Marriage Committee Members	Pastors	House Leaders	Total
Yes	6	2	9	6	23
No	2	3	7	28	40
Total	8	5	16	34	63

Source: Primary Data

Table 12.2.Expected frequency

Response	Vetting Committee Members	Marriage Committee Members	Pastors	House Leaders	Total
Yes	2.92	1.82	5.84	12.41	23
No	5.07	3.17	10.15	21.58	40
Total	6	5	16	34	63

Source: Primary Data

Hypothesis 13

Table 13.1.Observed frequency

Reponse	Vetting Committee Members	Marriage Committee Members	Pastors	House Leaders	Total
Yes	6	3	3	2	14
No	-	6	8	35	49
Total	6	9	11	37	63

Source: Primary Data

Table 13.2.Expected frequency

Response	Vetting Committee Members	Marriage Committee Members	Pastors	House Leaders	Total
Yes	1.33	2	2.44	8.22	14
No	4.66	7	8.55	28.77	49
Total	6	9	11	37	63

Source: Primary Data

Hypothesis 14

Table 14.1.Observed frequency

Reponse	Vetting Committee Members	Marriage Committee Members	Pastors	House Leaders	Total
Yes	6	2	9	6	23
No	2	3	7	28	40
Total	8	5	16	34	63

Source: Primary Data

Table 14.2.Expected frequency

Response	Vetting Committee Members	Marriage Committee Members	Pastors	House Leaders	Total
Yes	2.92	1.82	5.84	12.41	23
No	5.07	3.17	10.15	21.58	40
Total	6	5	16	34	63

Source: Primary Data